TOO MANY DOLLARS: TOO LITTLE SENSE

By

Paulette G. Honeygosky

**3000 spout run
arlington, va 22201**

ISBN: 0-75963-028-3

This book is printed on acid free paper.

1stBooks – rev. 4/4/01

TABLE OF CONTENTS

Foreword
Dedication

CHAPTER ONE
A VOTE WITHOUT REPRESENTATION   1

Term limits, gift rules, lobbying reforms and campaign finance proposals in 1994, 1995 and 1996 were pseudo-reforms at best. Democracy is at risk. Grassroots movements for genuine reform are long overdue.

CHAPTER TWO
HOW A LOBBY, FOR GOOD OR
ILL, BEGINS AND HOW IT GROWS   9

Lobbying is not a new phenomena. Nor is lobbying inherently an anti-democratic activity. On the contrary, both special interest groups and lobbyists are often helpful in promoting the common good in the legislative process. But the question now with us is: who will lobby those special interest groups and lobbyists who are corrupting the process in favor of the profit-makers?

CHAPTER THREE
TERM LIMITS: A SMALL STEP TOWARD REFORM:
DEALT A FEDERAL DEATH BLOW   12

In the past decade voters in twenty-four states put a referendum for state and federal term limits on the ballot. In twenty-three states the referendum passed. Voters overwhelmingly opted for a term of six years in the House and twelve years in the Senate for state and federal representatives.

In the summer of 1994 in the states of Washington and Illinois, the respective State Supreme Courts ruled against the citizens' right in those States to limit the elected official's right to run for a congressional office, and to run as many times as a candidate wished.

Subsequently, and contrary to the five years of citizen effort across the nation for a 6-12 form of federal term limits legislation [as proposed in the Inglis' amendment and then rejected], the House voted on March 29, 1995 on Resolution H.Res.73 [as proposed in the McCollum amendment] that would have allowed a congressional member to serve a term of twelve years in the House and twelve years in the Senate. House Resolution 73 was defeated by a vote of 227 to 204, with four legislators not voting.

Then in May of 1995 in the famed Arkansas case, the U.S. Supreme Court (as in the Washington and Illinois State Courts) ruled against the citizens' right to set federal office term limits, in favor of the Constitution that explicitly sets forth the requirements for U.S. House and Senate candidates for office.

CHAPTER FOUR
GRASSROOTS ELECTION REFORMS UNDERWAY 22

In many ways, voters in local communities engage in election reforms. Voters are learning to monitor and take charge of elections. They are organizing local forums and are questioning the candidates' qualifications. After the campaigning and voting is done, they continue to monitor the performance of their elected officials keeping an eye out for any undue influence that would tend to distort or corrupt the decision-making process.

Voters know that the key to being responsible employers is information. Knowing how their representatives vote, and letting them know how the voters want them to vote on an issue is important to the process.

CHAPTER FIVE
WHO SPOKE WHAT MESSAGE IN ELECTION '94? 33

In the November election of 1994 power shifted. The Republicans won a majority vote in both the House and the Senate. For forty years the Democrats had controlled the Congress but now the Democrats were in the minority.

Election analyists were stunned. No one had predicted this would happen. After the fact this writer, along with many others, offers an interpretation of why this power shift happened.

CHAPTER SIX
FUNDING FOR MILLION DOLLAR CAMPAIGNS   37

Term limits and lobbying reform legislation were steps on the way to campaign finance reform legislation. Voters know that special interest groups and their lobbyists know how to exploit the campaign finance "soft money loopholes" in the current system. In too many instances, they "legally" buy the legislators whose re-elections they finance.

CHAPTER SEVEN
REFORM PROMISES, PROMISES, PROMISES   45

Most folks today believe that the promises made by public officials are meaningless. Promises make great television sound bytes. But after the elections take place and the cameras are turned off, nothing changes. The promises made in the *Contract with America* was a case in point. Promises, promises, promises, - but nothing changed. Who will restore sense to the senseless?

CHAPTER EIGHT
VOTERS ARE CYNICAL   50

Reluctantly, the Senate brought the Term Limits issue to the floor [April 23, 1996] for a straight up and down vote on H.J. Resolution 21, a joint resolution proposing a constitutional amendment to limit congressional terms. No one expected the motion to pass. But everyone [especially the voters in those states where term limit legislation had been passed over the past several years; Perotians; Buchannanites, and others seeking political fodder for their reelection campaign literature] waited with bated breath to see how each Senator would vote the issue. But no vote happened. The proposal was scuttled by the Democrats' filibuster.

Elections, local and national, are bought and sold. The public was not fooled by the reform legislation proposed in '94, '95, '96, '98. The public is not fooled by the fact that reform legislation has little meaning. Public cynicism and disillusionment grow by the day.

A comprehensive movement, for the right of the Electors to due representation and the right of the Elected to be free to represent their constituents, cannot be far away. Anything more, or anything less, is politics at its worst. It is lobbyistic tyranny. To vote without due representation is the same as to allow the lobbyists and their wealthy employers to continue to tread on the rights of both the Electors and the Elected.

FOREWORD

I've written this book out of concern for what democracy increasingly is not. Government has failed in what I care most about. Today the poor get poorer. The rich get richer. The lowest fifth of America's population struggles to survive on 3.2% of the national income while the highest one-fifth luxuriates on 45.8% of the national income. No wonder that social injustice and the criminal elements in our society prevail, and that both racism and isolationism have resurfaced.

Everywhere there is unmistakeable evidence that it is the well-heeled special interest groups who are deciding public policy. It is clear from the evidence that campaign finance funders and their lobbyists now decide how legislation is written, what legislation is passed, and what budget cuts are made. It matters less and less who is elected to public office. It is the lobbyists who are today's legislators.

From both sides I've looked at the issues and observed the deleterious effects in the lives of ordinary folks as a result of senseless budget cuts and skewed national priorities. I've struggled to understand why this is so. I've talked the talk, lectured, written *Letters to the Editors* and letters to congressional leaders in behalf of a better life for the poor, the elderly and the oppressed. I have walked the walk when for more than twelve years, I did neighborhood development work, and taught empowerment to the powerless. I then mistakenly decided that even the best grassroots reform efforts were not good enough and that the solution to neighborhood problems rested with Congressional legislators.

So I left the local community scene and came to Washington to work in a lobbyist's office. While living and working in the Nation's Capitol, I have come to understand that lobbyists and special interest groups with access to unlimited wealth make government and its elected officials work for them. How they do this is described in what I have written in "Too Many Dollars; Too Little Sense".

The system is broke and it needs fixing. Elected officials who are bought and caught within the system cannot legislatively fix it. Having come full circle, I now believe that only a *National Reform Movement To Restore The Rights of both the Electors and the Elected* can wrest the power from the lobbyists and return both voice and vote back to the people; restore integrity to the election process, and enable candidates with ability and commitment to campaign and to win an elected office.

DEDICATED TO

Joseph & Anne (ne Spock) Honeygosky

MY PARENTS,

> GRASSROOT POLITICIANS IN THE BEST SENSE OF THE WORD, WHO USED GOOD COMMONSENSE TO GET OUT THE LOCAL VOTE IN THE CITY OF CLAIRTON, PENNSYLVANIA & TO ELECT PUBLIC OFFICIALS, WHO WERE CONCERNED FOR A BETTER QUALITY OF LIFE FOR THOSE WHOM THEY REPRESENTED

AND TO THE MEMORY OF THE LATE

Frank MacConnell, Jr.

> WHO, AT A NEW HAMPSHIRE TOWN MEETING ON JUNE 11, 1995, ASKED PRESIDENT CLINTON & HOUSE MAJORITY LEADER GINGRICH TO CREATE A NON-PARTISAN COMMISSION FOR THE SOLE PURPOSE OF GIVING THIS NATION - TRUE, AUTHENTIC, & MUCH NEEDED CAMPAIGN FINANCE REFORM. BOTH GENTLEMEN AGREED. IT HAS NOT YET HAPPENED.

A VOTE WITHOUT REPRESENTATION

In the District of Columbia the residents complain that though they are U.S. citizens, taxpayers, and live in the Nation's Capitol, they have no elected Senator or Representative in the Congress. They have no vote. They have no voice in this democracy described as of, by, and for the people. This is indeed a sad state of legislative affairs. It raises the fundamental democratic question of taxation without representation.

But what is perhaps even more tragic is that the rest of us, who do have a vote, and a Senator, and a Representative, either do not know or do not care that we, too, have little representation. We need to change this situation.

The effect of our vote on legislation and public policy is increasingly diminished. Between the voter and needed reforms are layers of "bought and paid for" legislators, committees and subcommittees to whom only funders and well-heeled lobbyists (lawyers for the most part) have access.

In a recent editorial "Congress Re-Entrenches"[1] Joseph Califano, who served as an aide to Lyndon Johnson, and who also served in Jimmy Carter's cabinet, is quoted as saying to C-SPAN, "Many members [of committees] are more loyal to the [funding] interests behind their committees than to their constituents".

Policy and budget priorities are no longer defined by the voters.Instead, policy is legislated because of voices that lobby with many dollars and, quite often, too little sense. America is fast becoming a democracy by and for the wealthy in behalf of the special interests of the wealthy. Real people with real problems no longer count. Few legislators care about real people who are old, real people who are poor, real people who have for several generations made a living growing grapes, corn, or raising chickens on their small family farms. Instead, powerful lobbies are in charge of legislation and of legislators and are destroying American life as real people know it.

The more this is so, the less democratic we are, and the less democracy we experience as individuals and as a nation. Voting statistics indicate that 62.2% of eligible voters in the November 1994 elections, did not bother to go to the polls and vote. Perhaps they no longer believed their votes make a difference.

The other 37.8% who did vote, did they really believe their vote can make a difference? Wake up, America. Look at the legislative charades in the two years since the 1994 election. Little that is positive was done. Much that is deleterious has happened. The presidential vetoes were indeed many. But history may yet record that these vetoes effectively prevented this Congress from abandoning the best in its own legislative history of budget priorities, environmental regulations, and public policies which were achieved with blood, sweat and tears by former legislators in the century now ended. [The end-game of the 104th Congress was

1

appalling. For example, with only four weeks remaining before Congress adjourned prior to the August national conventions, with not a single appropriations bill passed, the House was considering a Bill to lower inspection standards for poultry, in favor of profits for the poultry industry.] That is the way it was; it is the bad news and it is the sad news about representation for both the voter and the consumer.

Americans have the right to vote. Americans have struggled to give this right to vote to each other, regardless of sex, color,or creed. But many of us are now discovering that the vote we cast has little value in a democracy where dollars, not votes, make the difference in what legislation is introduced and passed by our elected representatives.

Early on, the Clinton administration recognized this and urged reform. In his *State of the Union* address on the night of January 15, 1994, President Clinton said, "It [the reforms this administration proposes] will raise critical questions about the way we finance our campaigns and about how lobbyists wield their influence. The work of change, frankly, will never get any easier until we limit the influence of the well-financed special interest groups who profit from the current system. So I also must now call on you [the Congress] to finish the job both houses began last year, by passing tough and meaningful campaign finance reform and lobby reform legislation this year".

Unfortunately, when a lobbying reform bill did reach President Clinton's desk in the Spring of 1994, it was weak and without substance.[2] The lobbying reform bill that passed the House by a vote of 315-110 in March 1994, for example, simply banned meals, entertainment and other such gifts from lobbyists to the lawmakers. It said nothing about pork-barrel spending written into legislation in favor of special interests. It said nothing about the tens of thousand *soft money* dollars (in kind contributions) from special interests to re-election campaigns. The Senate version of the reform bill also said nothing of substance on the issues. The end product in both Houses of Congress was inane.

Those who drafted the 1994 lobbying reform legislation didn't get it. But why should they? The very notion of lobbying reform legislation, properly drafted and voted into law, would put their lives and their jobs and their wealth on the line. "What About Reform for Congress", was a question raised in an editorial in the *Washington Post*.[3] The writer noted that the problems are clear. It costs millions to run for the House and Senate. Those running have to raise too much from too many groups that have a direct interest in legislation. These groups favor incumbents, since incumbents tend to win, and incumbents tend to win because they are favored by the interest groups. This trend is a comfort if you happen to be in the loop. It is vicious if you happen to be out.

In addition to the weak Lobbying Reform Bill of 1994, the House and Senate also passed Campaign Finance Reform Bills in the same year. Both bills were flawed. The two versions of the bill could have been brought together in a compromise legislative package that would have produced a better way of doing the public's business. The campaign spending limits in the House Bill needed to be tightened. The Senate Bill needed to authorize increased spending to adequately cover its proposed public funding requirements. Neither version of the bill included a secure and adequate way of financing campaign reform. Had these bills been put together by the conferees, they might have. No matter, Congress would still need to appropriate whatever money the final version of an effective campaign finance reform bill would have required. Congress showed no such intent. The compromise Bill, reported out of conference, did not pass. It made little difference. The Bill was devoid of the kind of legislative substance that makes for true reform.

The 103rd Congress in 1993-94 also had its chance with a Democratic majority in both Houses to cut through the frustration, pass real campaign finance and lobbying reform, and thus contribute significantly to an improved State of the Union. It did not do so.

Neither did the Republican majority in the 104th Congress do so even though its reform charades before the television cameras continued well into the final weeks of the session. It is significant though that the 104th Congress, early on, decided to deal with reform of the system at three levels, which indicates that Congress knew well what the problems were. First, the 104th Congress saw the need for legislating a ban on gifts to legislators; second, saw the need for legislating for more complete lobbying disclosure, and finally, saw the need for legislating for campaign finance reform. Congress, then and now, knows that the latter is the real problem. But the 104th Congress, like every Congress since, also knew that to deal with campaign finance reform is political suicide.

Step one and two were achieved. Token reforms were put in place. But step three, campaign finance reform measures, were nowhere in evidence.

Step one. Both the House and Senate passed gift ban rules in 1995. Rule 52 adopted in the House on November 16, 1995 and effective January 1,1996 bans all gifts regardless of value unless they are gifts from family, from a fellow member of Congress, or from friends and only when the gift is an expression of friendship and not offered as a means to curry influence. The Senate Rules said that only a gift (including lunch invitations) with a value of less than fifty dollars, and no more than a hundred dollars in gifts per year from a single source, may be accepted.

A "joke" was the insider's word on the Hill used to describe these new gift rules adopted by the 104th Congress that even at best failed to include meaningful accountability and enforcement provisions. [Moreover, even as we write, there are serious in-house differences of opinion on what these Gift Rules stipulate. Clarifying memos continue to emerge from the House Committee on Standards of Official Conduct - issued "to refine and supplement" the Rules.]

Step two. The House proposed a lobbying disclosure reform bill, H.R.2564. This House Bill was tabled. Subsequently, the Senate lobbying reform bill, S.1060, was passed in the Senate and then sent to the House where it was also passed. It was signed into law on December 19, 1995 by President Clinton and it became effective on January 1, 1996. It did amend the lobbying reporting and registration requirements that had been in effect since 1946. This new law known as the Lobbying Disclosure Act of 1995 describes a lobbyist as: any one who is working twenty percent of the day on lobbying activities, and who makes more than one "lobbying contact" written or oral with the legislative personnel covered in the legislation. A third criterion under this law is that the individual lobbyist spends $5,000, a group spends $20,000, on lobbying activities. Given that all three criteria are met, registration as a lobbyist is required. Initial registration as a lobbyist under this new law was set for February 14, 1996. Registered lobbyists are required to report bi-annually as to how they raise funds; who on the Hill they visit, for what purpose, and to whom they give funds. Fines of up to $50,000 may be levied against violators who fail to report the above. (There is little evidence this will occur.)

This Bill gives little hope for reform. It is problematic. The Bill was intended to disclose who is being paid how much, by whom, to influence which issues. As passed, the bill did little in any of these areas. At best the Bill will numerically identify more lobbyists than the 1946 law did. It doesn't do enough in terms of disclosure and accountability. The spin on the legislation was that emphasis on disclosure would discourage genuine grassroots' activism. Left unsaid was the fact that powerful lobbying groups (e.g. the National Rifle Association and the tobacco lobby) supported the legislative agenda of the Republican majority in the 104th Congress.

Consequently, contacts and lobbying activities were not carefully defined in the Bill. Word about town, then and now, is that the registration form (that defines who is required to file), and the report forms to be filed by registered lobbyists every six months, are subject to very broad in-house interpretation. This suggests that the report forms end up as negligible. They admit to little. The problems in the future as in the past is this law's weak accountability and enforcement provisions. Without such provisions, none of it adds up to meaningful lobbying reform.

There also is in this new lobbying law a controversial provision that prohibits lobbying by non-profit groups with federal contracts. The language is ambivalent.[4,5] It bars any group, that receives federal funding, from spending more than 5% of its budget on lobbying.[6,7] In no shape or form can this provision in the bill be called reform. It was a ruse. It effectively silenced those groups whose budgets were to be cut in the 104th session of Congress. Many of the newly elected House members insisted on this provision in the Bill.

Otherwise they threatened to block passage of the Senate-passed Bill when it returned for the final vote on the House floor.

This prohibitive language in the Bill is known as the Istook Amendment because it was Istook the Congressman from Oklahoma who presented it. It limited groups which receive a third of their total revenue in federal funds to spend no more than $100,000 of their private funds for political advocacy. Among the groups affected by this provision in the Bill was the AARP that ostensibly protects the rights of the nation's elderly. Another group affected was the Blue Cross/Blue Shield lobby, organized to protect the insurance coverage of millions, and among whom are the vast majority of federal employees.

A third group upset by the anti-lobbying provision in this Bill, Catholic Charities USA, was among the signers of a letter to then House Speaker Newt Gingrich and former Senate Majority Leader Robert Dole, saying that the proposal would "tie our hands and stifle our voices". Whether these anomalies in the lobbying disclosure law will ever be resolved one day, given today's climate of zeal for the right of free speech, remains to be seen.

Step three. The third category of reform - campaign finance reform - was legislatively in this session of Congress all over the lot. Most of the bills suggested caps on campaign spending and campaign giving. There was much ado before the tv cameras, but nothing of substance happened. In the House there were six Bills: HR 296; HR 732; HR 1427; HR 1837; HR 2307 and HR 2573. These bills, one by one, died in committee. But the fact that there were so many campaign finance reform bills introduced in the House indicates the vast diversity of opinion on this issue. [Gingrich indicated on *Meet the Press* on July 14th, 1996 that a reform bill would reach the House floor for a vote before Congress recessed for the summer. It did not. It didn't matter.) Like the gift rules and the lobbying disclosure law, these House campaign reform bills were inconsequential both in content and enforcement provisions.

In the Senate there were several campaign finance reform bills: S.46; S.1219 and S.1389. These proposed Senate Bills were in the Senate Rules & Regulations Committee. They differed slightly from the House bills in that they at least raised the possibility of partial public funding of election campaigns, suggested changes in the law that would close some of the loopholes, and attempted to limit *soft money* (both dollars and in kind contributions, such as use of company jets, limo service, etc.).

But few believed that any genuine campaign finance reform legislation would come out of any of the House or Senate Committees in 1996, primarily because 1996 was a presidential election year and campaign finance money was the name of the game.

In addition to the new Gift Rules, the Lobbying Disclosure Bill, and the futile attempts at Campaign Finance Reform legislation, there were in 1995 a few other cosmetic reforms happening on the Hill where lobbyists by the hundreds freely roamed the office buildings. In the past each lobbyist had a special identification card that allowed unlimited access to the congressional halls. But in the summer of 1995 these I.D.s were recalled. Lobbyists now could only access the congressional halls by special invitation.

Was this done for security reasons or for crowd control? Or is this an - only if you fund me, you influence me - attempt by the legislators to share in the lobbyists' [and the lobbyists' employers'] wealth? At best, it is cosmetic reform. It doesn't amount to much.

Another questionable practice, yet to be reformed, has to do with the public hearings convened by the various House and Senate committees. The long-standing practice is that lobbyists pay "waiters", who are usually university students, to wait on the Hill through the night and into the early morning, until the doors open. The paid "waiter" then stands in line and is ticketed for a seat in the hearing room. A few minutes before the hearing begins, the lobbyist shows up, pays the "waiter" for the ticket and then takes the ticketed seat in the hearing room. At several hundred dollars a ticket, about eleven dollars an hour is earned by the waiter. Another nineteen an hour is paid to the entrepreneur agency. (This practice is both the in-line-waiter and the entrepreneur's dream come true.) At this price the hearings are often attended only by lobbyists. The ordinary citizen, who doesn't have the dollars to spare, has little opportunity to attend a public hearing on the Hill. This is yet another example of the current abuse of power that needs reform.

In my opinion, the House or Senate lobbying and campaign finance reform bills, as proposed or passed [in 1994-1996], and the cosmetic reforms made during that timeframe, provide very little relief. No proposal demonstrated real determination on the part of the 104th Congress to reform the system. Each attempt was somewhat like the lion in the Wizard of Oz. Each gave evidence of the lack of a courageous political heart.

As a Washington semi-insider, I am convinced that reform, when it comes, will need to come from a National Movement to Restore the Rights of Electors and the Elected, that would at least include partially publicly-financed campaigns. There are such movements in many states where folks know that publicly-financed campaigns will wrest power from special interest groups and return it to the people. Such campaigns can give to the cities, the states, the nation, - public servants free to govern in the interests of the voters who elect and employ them. The influence of the funders, who now control the decisions of state assemblies, local town council meetings, and the Houses of Congress, would be considerably weakened.

Time and again, voters have pressed for a particular decision, only to learn that the decision had already been made in a back room by the person writing the biggest check. Voters have learned that the public meeting is a facade.

Discussion at the meeting, if any, does not really matter. No one is listening. The decision has been bought and pre-paid for.

On the local scene, voters are able to see this happening; they are able to question the priorities of government. But at the federal level there is no discernible connection between good legislation that never sees the light of day, and poor legislation that is passed into law. Voters do not immediately see that, in practice, the connection lies with the wealth of the campaign funders, who in a carefully orchestrated manner, control the legislator and the legislation their interest does or does not support. For example, when insurance companies wanted the Medical Saving Accounts (MSA's) written into health legislation, their lobbyists went into action. The health legislation proposed was substantially good in that it assured portability of health benefits from one employer to another. It also assured health benefits during the first six months of unemployment.

Lobbyists pressured for MSA's to be tacked onto this legislation, not out of concern for better health coverage, but as a way to allow the insurance companies to make huge profits. (The Kennedy filibuster was an attempt to force separate votes on Portability [a good] and MSA accounts [one of the so-called legislative poison pills].)

Had the legislation passed, (It did not.) those who opted for MSA's and remained healthy, and the insurance companies who would have administered the four thousand dollars a year that employers [or Medicare] would deposit in the name of each beneficiary, would benefit considerably. For the employee or retiree who participated and remained relatively healthy, the MSA's would become a second or third tax-exempt retirement fund since a portion of the funds not used to cover health costs would escrow to their retirement fund. For the insurance companies the MSA's would become very profit-making investment funds. Their concern, for profits sake, would be the maintenance of the health of the healthy, not health care for the ill; at will, again for profits sake, they could decide that a procedure was unnecessary and would not be covered under the MSAs.

But for persons who, because of choice; unemployment; or employers unable to offer MSA coverage, would not participate in the MSA's, they would suffer the consequences. Their non-MSA insurance premiums would sky-rocket even as the benefits under their health policy [Medicare or privately-funded coverage] would be diminished.

Other examples of a travesty of truth via lobbyism have come to light. None is more poignant than a recent exposé by a tobacco lobbyist, when he learned he had cancer of the throat and lungs. Facing impending death, he began to speak out on primetime television. He told the world how, for the sake of wealth, power, and job security, he had falsified the data when he testified that smoking had been proven not to cause cancer.

This admission in 1995 by a lobbyist is a sad commentary on the current state of legislative affairs. The tragedy is that the enormity of the influence wielded by the lobbyist on elected officials is little understood. And when it is understood, it is thought to be too entrenched in the system to be challenged.

But as a Washington observer of the political process, I believe the system can be challenged. Voters across this nation, who walk the walk, and talk the talk in their neighborhoods, cities, and states, can reform the system. Local voters see firsthand that the educational needs of their children are not being met. Local voters know that taxes are high yet public services are few.

When the local government's decisions are not in sync with reality, local voters can prod and pressure their public servants to be servants of the public who employ them. When this doesn't happen, they can vote them out of office.

Similar reform of the system on every level of governance is long overdue. The founding fathers of democracy, who wrote and enacted into law the Declaration of Independence and the Bill of Rights, were way ahead of their time. In their day it is true that only land-owning white males voted. In their day many of them were slaveowners. In their day many of them had sustained grave personal injustice under British rule. But,notwithstanding, they were men with a vision of a better world. They had the political courage to give us the inherent promise of legislation that was to be - of, by, and for the people. They challenged us to create a better world than they themselves had experienced. They reminded us that each person is created equal under the law, and has an inalienable right to life, liberty, and the pursuit of happiness.

In the two hundred years that have followed their governance, creative reform legislation like that which they gave us when they wrote the Constitution and the Bill of Rights is indeed rare. Instead we have become a polarized nation and a polarized world of have and have nots. [Americans, for example, consume 48% of the world's resources and yet constitute only 6% of the world's population.] Why? One reason: the election of our legislators depends on the lobbyists' campaign financing. Our legislators are not guided by intelligence, compassion, and the principles of sound governance. As bought and paid for, they are selling themselves and this nation short. Our humanity is diminished. Politically, we are our own worst enemy.

Such abuse of power by *bought and paid for* legislators, so many of whom remain in power for decades, were it to remain unchallenged by the voter, puts this nation, this world and the future of democracy at serious risk.

HOW A LOBBY, FOR GOOD OR ILL, BEGINS AND HOW IT GROWS

Notwithstanding the abuse of power by many special interest lobbyists, there are lobbies that were originally created for the common good, and were, and are, essentially well meaning and useful. One such example is the American Association of Retired Persons.

"In 1958", says Lindley H. Clark, Jr. in "How The Biggest Lobby Grew", a January 17, 1994 commentary,[8] "when Ethel Percy Andrus, a retired high school principal, founded the AARP, neither she nor anyone else could have known exactly what she was starting." In 1947, Ethel Andrus set up the National Retired Teachers' Association to deal with the tax, pension, and insurance problems of its members. Because it was successful, she decided to extend the idea to older Americans. Andrus worked at the AARP until she died in 1967. Before and after her death,the association she founded grew phenomenonally.

The AARP now has thirty-three million members. When AARP lobbies an issue, it speaks numerically and qualitatively loud and clear, and Washington listens.

In the Spring of 1996, the tax-exempt status of the AARP, and the federal dollars it receives, was the subject of congressional hearings. The 104th Congress claimed AARP used federal funds to lobby against the federal government. Specifically, Congress questioned AARP's 501 (c)4 status which allows it to lobby as a "social welfare organization", so long as the principal purpose of its lobbying is to advance social welfare.

The congressional hearings were a smokescreen. They were part of the strategy of the Republican-controlled Congress to budget major cuts in medicare funding and to incrementally end the Medicare system as we know it. [A few non-partisan voices, like that of R. Randolph Richardson, president of the Smith Richardson Foundation, agreed with this Congress. Richardson suggested that in defining "social welfare", AARP had shown unusual disregard for the opinions of its members. Richardson went on to suggest that AARP lobbied in favor of the Clinton health plan, for example, because the plan exempted mail-order pharmaceutical firms from the cost controls imposed on ordinary pharmacies. AARP, noted Richardson, has a stake in pharmaceutical mail-order firms, considered by many as its cash cow in that retirees order their medications from AARP, which in turn purchases in bulk from the mail order pharmacies.]

But the AARP leadership, masters of political action and brilliant at organizing media events, did not bow to such criticism; they were neither silent nor subtle at the congressional hearings. They let Congress know that the elderly across this nation will in the end have the last word when they vote their opposition to proposed medicare reforms, and vote their displeasure with the congressional investigations of AARP.

The AARP is a fundamentally sound lobby. But there are less sound interest groups whose lobbyists are former elected officials after a lucrative job change, who monitor public policy with an eye for business profits for themselves or their employers.[9] One such job-seeking lobbyist [Glenn English], quoted in "Former Lawmaker Says Lucrative Job As Lobbyist Offered Way Out of Congress",[10] said that even though he knew he would be criticized heavily as many former lawmakers are, he would at least get a hefty raise from his $133,600 congressional salary. He knew his lobbyist predecessor had earned $230,000 and more.

In a lead article,[11] "For the Baby Bells, Government Lobbying Is Hardly Child's Play", Rick Hartman and John Howard offer an appreciable insight into the phone company's lobby. It is an article worth more than a cursory reading. It shows the muscle of a lobby, and describes the lobbyist's unlimited spending power. His employer's wealth gives the lobbyist the ability to shape industry regulation by government in such a way that the industry that employs them will net the greatest profits. The strategy is clear: finance the re-election campaign of a legislator. Instruct the industry's legal department to write the appropriate legislative provisions. Request the legislator to introduce these provisions as new legislation, or tack them onto a pending bill as an amendment. When passed into law, this legislation then allows the industry to net huge profits in its future transactions.

It is this type of dealmaking between the lobbyist and the legislator that explains why industry employs, often at a $450,000 salary or more, former government officials, who know the process by which a bill becomes public law. Industry knows that former legislators make very clever lobbyists.

Notwithstanding their categorical abuse of power, there are lobbyists, who find in the lobbying forum, a way to address the issues they would rather have resolved while they were in Congress. But when they were in Congress, they could not effectively make a difference, so entrenched was the power of the committee chairpersons and other power-holders within the system. The article quoted above bears this out when it says of the lobbyist under discussion that instead of battling to stave off budget cuts, he'll soon lobby old friends in Congress. In this way he will oversee the passage of legislation and appropriations for the new rural programs that he actually designed but could not successfully process while a legislator on Capitol Hill.

Many lobbyists, from the outside looking back, seem free-er to address reforms that as legislators in Congress, they knew were needed but were powerless to effect while working within the system. Former Congressman Tony Coelho, employed by the Gore presidential campaign until illness forced his retirement, has much to say about how he would change the system he left and that he knew so well. In a recent article,[12] he described the reforms he would recommend.

He suggests: 1. Limit service on congressional committees. 2. Automatically reorganize Congress every decade. 3. Reform campaign financing so that legislators deal more with substantive issues and less with raising campaign money.

In the same article he editorializes the issue of campaign finance reform and his own role in American politics. There hasn't been a better political fundraiser than Tony Coelho. Nobody knows more than he what a debilitating process fundraising is. The problem is not so much that contributors think they own you or industries control you, although there are examples of that.

Coelho's primary concern, the article notes, is the amount of time it takes for individuals to raise money. "I had a very close friend in the Senate who told me [Coelho] that in the two years prior to each re-election he would spend as much as 70% of his time raising money. That means he only could spend 30% of his time on the country's problems."

Campaign financing was the major concern of the thirteen Senators who retired from Congress in the same year as Bradley. On *Nightline* [December 13], Senator Bradley, a legislator of considerable stature made his concern public. Campaign fund-raising, he said, simply takes too much time away from the job of legislating. We must do something about the money and about campaign finance reform. Again, in his bid for the year 2000 presidency, he repeated this concern for campaign finance reform; he did not become the Democratic party's nominee.)

Senator Paul Simon reaffirmed this concern [December 17] even more boldly on *Meet the Press*. He minced no words when he said that we need to change the campaign finance laws so that "no election can ever again be bought".

Paulette G. Honeygosky

TERM LIMITS: A SMALL STEP TOWARD REFORM: DEALT A FEDERAL DEATH BLOW

Over the past decade there was a movement in state after state for term limit legislation. Twenty-three states opted for term limits. Among these states were: Alaska, Arizona, Arkansas, California, Colorado, Florida, Idaho, Louisiana, Maine, Massachusetts, Michigan, Missouri, Montana, Nebraska, Nevada, North Dakota, Ohio, Oklahoma, Oregon, South Dakota, Utah, Washington and Wyoming. Many other states were actively involved in the more than five years [1989-1995] struggle for term limit reform. In November, 1995, Mississippi was the 24th state to attempt to limit the terms of its state legislators but due to the mixed signals from the courts and the media at this time, the referendum in Mississippi was defeated.

Generally speaking, public opinion during this time favored a twelve year stint in the Senate. Public opinion for a six year limit in the House was divided. Most voters seemed to favor **six years** in the House and **twelve years** in the Senate.

Initially overruling public opinion on the issue of term limits were several decisions of the courts. When the voters of the state of Washington, for example, voted-in a measure to restrict a Senate term to twelve years, and a House term to six years, a lawsuit was filed by a fourteen term Democratic Congressman. Tom Foley had held office for twenty-eight years. He would have been unable to run for a fifteenth term had the voters' referendum prevailed. But in the courts, Foley won.

The issue at stake was twofold: first, whether the voters of the state of Washington could exert power over the federal government by setting term limits for its congressional representatives. And secondly, whether the federal government could declare term limit legislation, passed by the voters of a state for its state and federal officials, non-binding for its federal officials.

Initially, new hope sprang up on both sides of the issue. By upholding the power and authority of a state to enact laws that would encourage or require rotation in office for their elected officials, many believed that the court's decision could breathe new life into the Founding Fathers' design of a federal system in which the states could provide a meaningful check on the powers of the central government. Such a court decision would insure that members of Congress would always know it is the states and the people, to whom the federal government is accountable, and not the other way around.

On the other hand, it was known by the voters that the alternative, much more difficult to achieve, to such a State Supreme Court decision if it was unfavorable to the voters of the state would be through an amendment to the U.S. Constitution.

Which would it be? Washington state's court decision was a test case. It was the first of a series of watershed moments in term limits judicial history. Where would resolution of the term limit issue come from? Would it come from an amendment to the Constitution? Would it come from term limit legislation as promised in the *Contract with America*? Or would it come from a State or Federal Supreme Court decision?

It's a matter of record that the Washington State Supreme Court decision was pro-Speaker Foley. Term limit advocates in the state of Washington lost. Washington state voters were told they could not limit the number of times their federal representatives could run for office.

In a thirty-nine page February 19, 1994 ruling in this Folian lawsuit,[13] Judge William Dwyer stated that term limits abrogate the voters' constitutionally guaranteed freedom of choice in electing their leaders. He went on to say that such limits are clearly directed at a "disfavored group of candidates". In this decision the Judge emphasized that term limits are aimed solely at veteran legislators. Who can say, he argued, whether future voters will reverse themselves, suddenly preferring experienced politicians to those new to the game and who would then petition the courts to re-write the rules.

Shortly thereafter, Judge Dwyer's prediction of such a reversal in the public's position on term limits, began to come true.[14] In some states, specifically New York[15] and Tennesse where term limits had successfully been voted in, elected officials of those states spent a great deal of the taxpayers' money to hold special elections and attempt to have the referendums overturned.

Fortunately or unfortunately, they did not succeed in doing so. In a few other states where terms limits would have been retroactive and would have affected **veteran** elected officials currently in office, the referendum on term limits did not pass. It seems voters wanted their cake and wanted to eat it, too. They wanted the good veteran legislators, but not the bad ones. But voters can't have it both ways. Notwithstanding, many proponents of term limits, boldly and without chagrin, insisted that term limits should apply to the newcomers and not to those veteran office holders whom they had learned to trust. There is something to be said for this stance. But we know that legislation, term limit legislation or otherwise, cannot be bent that way.

Following this setback occasioned by the Washington state court decision in the Spring of 1994, there was an Illinois State Supreme Court decision in early autumn of the same year, that simply removed the term limit referendum from the ballot. The Illinois Court gave no immediate legal opinion as to why it had so ordered. This Illinois Court decision had serious consequences.[16] In its August of 1994 decision the Court voted 4 to 3 to remove the term limit referendum that had been placed on the November ballot by more than 400,000 citizens of that State and was leading 68% to 22% in the polls. In the aftermath of the Illinois State Supreme Court decision, the very title of the following day's lead editorial on the Court's decision described pretty much where the struggle for term limit legislation then was. The title read *Voters Be Damned*. The Illinois Supreme Court, like the Washington State Supreme Court, had legislated against the rights of a vast number of the voters in these respective states.

This Illinois State Supreme Court decision came in the early fall of 1994 when politics was at its lowest ebb. The House was attempting to defeat the Crime Bill, and the Senate was trying to defeat both the Crime and the Health Bills.

Much was happening at this time to give voters everywhere cause for concern. The National Rifle Association (NRA) and Labor were storming the congressional halls as never before in political history. Their presence *en masse* on the Hill was a prelude to the voter discontent that contributed to the shift in power in the November 1994 elections.

But it was the U.S. Supreme Court decision in May of the following year that dealt the judicial death blow to the movement for term limits legislation. This 5-4 decision struck down an Arkansas term limits law and effectively invalidated term limit legislation already passed in twenty-two other states. The Court ruled that states cannot legislate the requirements of office for a federal officeholder. (They can only do so for state officeholders.) The requirements for federal office holders are spelled out in the United States Constitution. Only an amendment to the Constitution, said the Court, can change these requirements.

The decisions of the Washington State Supreme Court and the Illinois State Supreme Court in 1994, and the U.S. Supreme Court in 1995, killed the movement for term limits. But the question for many is not whether there ought to be term limits. The question for many is still - how many years of public service at the state and federal level are we talking about. How long can a legislator effectively legislate before power that corrupts sets in? Most folks remember from experience that power tends to corrupt and that absolute power tends to corrupt absolutely.

Those members of Congress, who feared that term limits could still happen one future day by way of a constitutional amendment, tried to make a case for term limits by advocating terms as long as possible. This self interest was clearly evidenced in March of 1995, when the historic vote in the House on term limits was taken. Among the promoters of the longest terms possible were those congressional members who introduced and supported the Hilleary Amendment. This amendment proposed a cap of twelve years in both the House and Senate, but allowed the voters to make the final decision in the various States about how many years less than twelve their representatives would serve. It was non-retroactive. This amendment was defeated 164-265, with five legislators not voting.

Other House members supported the Inglis Amendment and argued for six years in the House and twelve years in the Senate, non-retroactive. This amendment also stated that a term is served in full if 50% of it is served. Though most favored by public opinion, this amendment was defeated 114-316, with four legislators not voting.

There was least support for the Democrats' Peterson-Dingell-Frank Amendment which stipulated twelve years of service in both the House and Senate and was retroactive.[17] The Democrats admitted it was a political anti-Gingrich joke. Gingrich had thrown his support for the McCollum amendment [which proposed 12 years in the House and 12 years in the Senate; non-retroactive]. Yet even as he was supporting this McCollum amendment in the House, Gingrich stood before the TV cameras and spoke publicly in support of the 6-12 proposal which he knew the vast majority of those who favored term limits were advocating. The Democrats knew this. They challenged the Gingrich private vs his public posture by introducing the Peterson proposal.

Who then would vote for the Peterson proposal? Not Gingrich, joked the Democrats. In the end, to no one's surprise, the Peterson amendment was defeated 135-297, with two legislators not voting.

The one amendment that was acceptable both to Gingrich and his colleagues was the McCollum amendment. It proposed twelve years in the House and in the Senate, non-retroactive, and it validated any and all previously adopted State-legislated term limits. But after considerable discussion, this amendment was withdrawn. No vote for or against it was cast. It died on the legislative vine and no explanation was given.

At the end of a long and confusing debate, the House Judiciary Resolution 73 that would have amended the U.S. Constitution was voted on. It proposed twelve years of service in the House and twelve years in the Senate, non-retroactive. It was rejected 204-227, with four legislators not voting. It fell 61 votes short of the two-thirds majority of those present and voting, that was necessary for a constitutional amendment to be passed. [If and when it had been passed in both Houses, this proposed amendment would still have to be ratified by two-thirds of the states. Only then would it have become an amendment of the Constitution.]

This vote in the House on a term limits Consitutional amendment was originally scheduled for March 14, 1995.[18] Again, with no explanation given, the vote was rescheduled for March 29th.[19]

The votes in the House for passage of term limits legislation were not there. An acceptable content in the legislation was not there either.[20]

Many believed that there would be less political fall-out if the issue of term limits was left to the U.S. Supreme Court's pending decision in the Arkansas case. Certainly it would be less politically costly for anyone who might be running for re-election.

Then like the direction of the wind, the mood in the House changed quickly. The feeling surfaced among the Republican members of the House that they ought to vote the issue even though they knew by their own pre-count that it would be defeated.

They also hoped the blame would be laid on the Democrats for not giving the issue their support.

No matter how it is explained, the term limit promise written into the *Contract with America* was broken. The recorded accounts of the defeat of this legislation do not tell the real story behind this reform charade. The real story involves the difference between what the *Contract* promised, and what the House members actually did with the legislation on the House floor [and, as we shall see, in the House Judiciary Committee].

The House never let the issue come to a final vote of passage in a straight-forward six-twelve piece of legislation [as proposed in the Inglis' amendment] even though most members knew this was what the voters wanted. That's why the vote on the twelve-twelve form was such a let down. Neither the mock debate, nor the failure to vote on a straight-forward six-twelve form of the legislation demonstrated a sincere effort at reform. It flaunted the wishes of the voters; right from the start; it set up a "let's pretend"/reform scenario,[21] that fooled no one.

The voters' trust in the *Contract* and its proponents was greatly diminished.

Following this pretense at reform and this defeat of term limits on the floor of the House, former Senator Dole promised in a television sound byte, ostensibly designed to quell the rising anger of the voters, that term limits legislation would be voted on in the Senate sometimes in early June,1995. [But the Senate vote on term limits was not scheduled until April 23,1996, at which time no vote ever occurred due to a filibuster by the Senate Democrats.]

Grassroots advocates, silent before the vote in the House, were once again upset by this no vote in the Senate. If there are to be term limits, let the reform be credible: twelve years in the Senate [two terms] and six years, not twelve, in the House [three terms]. In this, voters and their advocates were not just playing the numbers game. Voters across the states had overwhelmingly favored a three term limit in the House and a two term limit in the Senate. Of the twenty-three states that passed term limits, nineteen of them voted for less than a twelve year term limit for a House member.

It seemed clear to all, except the House legislators who voted down issue term limits on March 29, 1995, that most people strongly prefer a shorter limit for the House than in the Senate. This advocacy for a shorter limit for the House legislators has its basis in the belief of the Founding Fathers of this country who, as noted by Edward H. Crane in February 17,1994[22], believe in a citizen legislature. "If democracy is to work, legislators have to be of the people, representing the interests of what we now refer to as the private sector. To turn the House into a citizen legislature and to make it a true House of Representatives, we must attract people who prefer to spend their productive lives in the private sector and who view their time in Washington as a leave of absence from their real careers. As it is now, most people look at the prospect of running and recognize, first, that the odds of beating an incumbent are small, and second, that even if you do win, it will be a very long time before your opinion counts for anything under the [current] seniority system. Since most people aren't willing to buck those odds, our ballots are clogged with career politicians and with would-be careerists."

In states where term limit legislation already exists for elected officials, state legislatures are bubbling over with the creativity and idealism of their legislative novices, who simply take a leave of absence from their careers. They get into the system, try out a few reform ideas, and hope to make a difference. When such persons are in the majority, as they are in some States, we hear echoes in their debate of the creativity and commitment, that characterized the decisions of those who wrote the Constitution and founded this democracy more than two hundred years ago. They are legislators who legislate freely and responsibly.

Seeing the difference term limits make at the state level, there are many who are disillusioned with the performance of legislators, too long in office, and who believe that, not only at the state level but also on the federal level, America needs term limits.

They believe that America needs a grassroots' citizen legislature if we are again to be a vibrant democracy, creative, free of corruption, and free of undue lobbying and special interest pressures.

Voters see the need to level the political field of play so that the elected have a chance to create legislation that will restore the American dream.

The notion of term limits has been bandied about by both the Republican and the Democratic party leadership. However, neither party ever seemed intent on getting much beyond the rhetoric. It is not generally known, for example, that early-on in the first session of the 104th Congress [well before the March 29, 1995 floor vote on term limits], a brief had been filed by the Chairman of the House Judiciary Committee, where jurisdiction over the term limit issue resides. The brief cited the unconstitutionality of state-imposed term limits on the tenure of congressional representatives. Such a U.S. Supreme Court decision, if the premise were granted, would moot all legislative efforts for term limits.

Yet, in spite of this brief which they had already filed,[23,24] the House Republicans were out front, before the television cameras, and subsequently on the House floor, keeping up the facade, and pretending to support term limit legislation.

Senate members, who never signed the *Contract with America* are to this day publicly silent on the issue of term limits.

The Senate's hidden opposition to term limit legislation also began in the Senate Judiciary Committee. With little publicity, the term limit measure in the Senate Judiciary Committee, as in the House Judiciary Committee, was also considered in January, 1994. The Chairman of the Senate Judiciary Committee arbitrarily decided the issue was redundant. Term limit legislation would in his opinion show a fundamental lack of faith in the good judgment of the voters. So he dropped the item from the Committee agenda and it was therefore given no consideration by the Committee. That's pretty much where the term limit measure stood in the Senate until the Senate filibuster [and the no vote of the Senate] on April 23, 1996. The Senate resorted to the tactic, - ignore it and it may go away. There were a few remarks here and there. Bob Dole said before the cameras that he might vote for term limits. But to do so, he quickly added, would mean that small states like his own Kansas would lose the influence now enjoyed by lawmakers with seniority. (He had that notion right.)

So even though a vote for term limits was one of the pieces of legislation promised by the Republicans in their *Contract With America*, it's hard to see how Gingrich or Dole could really push for term limits, especially since the legislation would have been effective retroactively, and would have covered all seated members of Congress. Both Gingrich and Dole, and many powerful Republicans, had long ago exceeded three terms in the House and two terms in the Senate, respectively. Moreover, the Republicans, at last the majority party, would have been hard pressed to relinquish power after serving forty years as the minority party.

But something of term limits through the vote of the voters did happen in the November 1994 election. As a direct result of this election, more than 50% of the House and Senate members that year were elected to serve their first or second term. Statistically that meant that of the members serving in the House in 1994, only one hundred and twenty-one Democrats and ninety-one Republicans were elected before 1990. It's not as though there was a deliberate attempt on the part of the voters to oust long entrenched members. It simply happened. Voters across the nation voted their frustration with government. When the results were tallied, the voters discovered that something unexpected had happened. As one analyst said, we discovered that many of the *old bulls* on the Hill were gone, and there seemed to be new hope, youth, and creativity in the congressional air.

Unfortunately, these young'uns usually had little or no positive effect in the short run because the powerful committee chairmen were still in control. Because of seniority, the remaining *old bulls* still chaired the powerful committees where the mark-up and passage of key legislation happens, even as the young'uns that year debated the issues to their heart's content, to little or no avail in the media, and in the general sessions.

We did see though that in this first session of this Republican-controlled Congress that the young'uns in the House had an unprecedented effect on the process of governance. Unfortunately, it was mostly negative. The two government shut-downs, and the tenuous budget negotiations they initiated, didn't augur well for a balanced budget to be passed in this session of this Congress. Neither did it augur well for the passage of much of the legislation both promised and needed at this time. Inexperience and inordinate commitment blurred the vision of many congressmen. It was gridlock every step of the way. Even so, this is not to say that the effort for term limited legislators should ever be discounted or discontinued.

The House had put the issue to a vote.

The Senate had said it would also vote the issue but when the first Senate vote on term limits was scheduled in October of 1995, former Senator Dole removed it from the Senate roster because as he said, the advocates for term limits told him they didn't have the votes to support it. [Then, as we have seen, the vote was rescheduled on April 23, 1996, when again it did not occur.] Another chapter in the comedy of pretense had happened in Congress!

The November 1994 elections suggest the way the voters responded in the next election to these term limit court decisions and to all the congressional broken promises. When the elected, young or old, experienced or inexperienced do not serve responsibly, then the electorate will simply vote them out of office. In the 1994 mid-term elections, voters rediscovered their power to do just that. So it's highly probable that term limits by the vote of the people, rather than term limits by legislation, or by court decisions, or by constitutional amendment, will remain the operative dynamic, at least in the foreseeable future.

Taking the long-range view, it would also seem that in state after state, the grassroots movement to write term limits into legislation or into the Constitution will not go away. Even in that unprecedented November 1994 mid-term election when the power in Congress shifted from the Democrats to the Republicans, term limits was on the ballot in eight states and also in the District of Columbia. In each instance, term limits was approved by a healthy margin.[25] As of November 28, 1994, twenty-two states had successfully voted for state and federal term limits.[26] Since that time the number has risen to twenty-three.

Understandably, current office holders particularly at the federal level do not support term limits, although most of them are careful not to say so publicly.[27] In a few rare instances, however, several politicians were willing to be honest about the issue, pro and con. Speaker Foley of the House will go down in history as someone who publicly opposed term limits. While in office, he blocked every House vote or hearing on term limits. He also petitioned the Washington State Supreme Court to rule against the voters' referendum which directly impacted his right to run for a fifteenth term. He then asked the court for taxpayer reimbursement of the legal expenses he incurred in opposing the term limit referendum.

All of this Folian folly backfired in the subsequent election when voters simply voted Foley out of office, no matter what the courts said or did about the anti-Foley term limit issue they had raised. Foley was one of the first Speakers of the House to go down and out of office so infamously and he is the first House Speaker in one hundred and thirty-two years to lose a bid for re-election.

The grassroots effort for term limits continued to spread throughout the land. In an interesting aside and at the height of the March 1995 term limits debate Albert R. Hunt advised the Democrats in Congress to counter the Republicans' term limits proposed legislation with a term limits proposal of their own.[28] Hunt suggested that the Democrats should advocate setting limits on committee chair assignments, rather than on the number of terms served, to assure a steady infusion of new ideas into the legislative process without losing institutional memory.

Contrary to his advice, the Democrats made no such motion. Term limit legislation was defeated in the House by a large majority of both Republicans and Democrats, Neither party really supported the issue. Gingrich continued to promise that it would be an issue in the '96 presidential elections. Forbes, Buchanan, and Perot also said it would. It was not.

But term limits remains a serious political issue simply because the Republicans believe that it was the term limits movement across the nation, together with the Religious Right, that helped give them the majority in both Houses of Congress. No matter whether this is true or not, it is true that these movements represent a large percentage of voters.

Whatever happens legislatively in the future, neither party and no legislator will ever hold office for forty or more years again. The genie is out of the box. The process is open.

In fifteen states in the fall of 1996, (even after the Arkansas Federal Court decision dealt the death blow to term limits) voters were being asked to vote for an initiative on the ballot that would instruct their legislators to call for a convention for the sole purpose of proposing a term limits amendment to the Constitution. Those legislators who chose not to commit to supporting such a convention had the word "Disregarded Voters' Instruction on Term Limits" placed next to their name on the ballot.

Legislators know that voter pressure is on. The eyes and ears of the voters are now open. The votes of the voters of the future will no longer be bought or job-controlled. Votes will be merited. Holding public office will be seen as a privilege and a responsibility.

Voters across the nation have learned to chant: "In November, we'll remember". Voter empowerment has set in for the duration.

Paulette G. Honeygosky

GRASSROOTS ELECTION REFORMS UNDERWAY

Aware that without campaign finance reform this country is in serious trouble, there is along with the movement for term limits, a grassroots effort for comprehensive election reform underway at many local levels all over America. Despite great hardship to the taxpayers, local campaigns for mayors, council members, and school board directors are now publicly financed.

At these local levels, where campaigns are financed by the taxpayer, the voters watch and wait for the difference. Voters are looking for, surprisingly finding, and electing to office, a new quality of leadership and governance. Voters are finding enthusiasm, creativity, and commitment in the political arena, - very rare qualities in public forums.

Moreover, local candidate forums are now held before every election, in each and every district, as close to and as accessible to each voter as possible. A candidate for public office is asked to stand before the local community that he or she wishes to represent and present a platform. Who and what the candidate stands for, and what the candidate proposes to do, is more important than how much money the candidate can raise for the party. Why the candidate wants to hold a public office becomes more important than who wants the candidate to hold that particular office for personal or corporate gain.

In these local communities, what the voters have going for them in their effort to reform and take back the system is access to the most powerful weapon ever wielded, - factual information. Since the 1992 elections, voters have access to reliable, hard and fast, factual information, unedited and without spin by the candidates or by their campaign staff. This information is available to the voter in their homes, instantly and low-cost, on the various online computer networks.

By tracking the voting records and the campaign finance histories of their elected representatives, voters can now hold their employees, particularly the incumbents, accountable to the taxpayers. The taxpayers can, if they will, begin to act as responsible employers.

Voters are learning that there is but one way to keep democracy healthy: keep an eye on the persons elected to office to make sure their representatives are not working for some special interest or for personal gain. Computer literate voters can do this. They are closely monitoring the officials they elect into office.

The 1992 elections reversed a thirty-year decline in voter participation. The voter's desire to participate in policy and budget decisions is gaining momentum. There is today almost immediate public reaction to presidential appointments, to congressional budget cuts, to policy shifts, and to the way individual members of Congress vote on policy issues.

Easy access by computer and fax to immediate information on both the issue and the voting records of the legislators is among the primary reasons why this is so. Most Americans today are well informed about the way government works. They have decided it is time to assert their claim to the ownership of government, and to take responsibility for making democracy work for them.

If there is any influencing to be done, the voters and taxpayers should be doing it, not lobbyists and special interest groups.

Voters are learning to go in person to see their public officials; to attend public meetings and present their views; to send e-mail messages, and to fax their concerns to the President, Vice-President, members of Congress, the Governor, and state legislators.

More importantly, voters are learning to vote carefully and wisely, intent on electing to public office, employees who will do the most good, for the most people.

In many communities across this land, both the elected and the electorate are standing tall. It's a new day for the implementation and experience of the democratic way of governing and the democratic way of life.

Hopefully voters across the nation learned to value their right to vote even more when they watched the first democratic elections in the land of Mandela. Telecasts of the elections in South Africa showed voters, some eighty or ninety years old, who stood in line for days without food or sleep and waited to exercise their right to vote. After a lifetime of struggle against the ills of apartheid, the South Africans knew it was both a right and a privilege to vote. They had earned that right. No matter their hunger or the inclement weather or the threat of violence, they waited in line. By week's end, in village after village, almost without exception, every eligible adult had voted.

In July, 1996, the first democratic election of a President was held in Russia. Here, too, voters, many of whom had personally sufferred under Communist dictators, risked for democracy, and voted into office Yeltsin and their hope for a new future. We can't go back is what their vote said.

Voters everywhere are beginning to see the difference their vote can make. They wish to vote for public officials, who when confronted with an issue, carefully consider the matter, and then make decisions that will benefit most people, most of the time. They no longer wish to vote for public officials, who are controlled by outside interests or personal gain or both. If to do that takes higher taxes to fund campaigns, then so be it. The end result will be governance that is democracy at its best. What is important is that each voter is beginning to understand that he or she is an employer and that public officials are employees of the voters. Voters are paying the bills. That means that public officials should hear from voters often. What employer would hire an employee and would then not be around to monitor and evaluate the employee's performance?

Voters should contact their representatives and express opposition to or support of a bill. Voters should keep the relationship between employer and employee active and responsible. If voters simply vote and pay taxes, it's not enough. If voters never know how their representatives and senators are representing them, it's not enough. If voters know, but never tell their elected officials how to represent them, it's not enough. Voters would then be guilty of mismanagement and irresponsibility and have no basis for complaining about how the government is being run.

As in any complicated system, voters are learning that democracy, to be vibrant and healthy, requires a willingness to maintain and evaluate it through periodic check-ups and constant attention to problems that may occur. Even as they are concerned with the health of their physical bodies, voters need to work to assure the health of their political bodies.

As employers, voters have two essential tasks:

1. To hire their employees wisely by first demanding that they describe in great detail how they will do the job of governing, if elected; and, 2. To supervise their employees after they are elected in order to make sure they are doing the job they were hired to do.

We know that lobbyists, much as we may wish them away, are constantly on the alert regarding the interest or issue they lobby. Voters can learn from the lobbyist's methods. Lobbyists read the literature. They listen to news. They read the fine print in the *Congressional Record* and the *Federal Register*. They visit the legislative and other appropriate information-sharing forums. They network by phone and fax. They are in constant touch with the legislators and their staffers, trying to urge the passage or the defeat of a piece of legislation, which they feel might even remotely affect the interest or issue they are employed to lobby.

Voters can learn from this persistence on the part of the lobbyist. Voters need to be just as informed and just as alert to any aspect of a piece of legislation, that suggests a policy change or allows the spending of public money, that, now or subsequently, would not be in their best interest.

A case in point is the congressional effort to draft and pass a balanced budget. The key to understanding this dilemma is information. Voters should do their research. Television staffers and newspaper reporters do not tell us the whole of what is happening. There is a great deal of fine print in the appropriation bills. It is only the fine print that will tell us that the proposed budget is actually legislating away nutrition, health, education, and environmental benefits that are needed by children and the elderly today and in the future, in favor of tax cuts for the wealthy. Voters cannot allow such a travesty of the political process to happen.

To monitor and promote legislation that will benefit most people, most of the time is difficult. It is almost impossible to do this on a national scale. The issues need to be brought to the local level and designed legislatively to address local interests. Voters in particular districts need to know who their representatives are and what they are proposing and voting for in legislative sessions. They need to hold them to the highest standards in favor of the common good. If each voter took on this task locally and responsibly, we would begin to have public officials on the national level aware who their employers are. They would then shape up or ship out.

This won't happen locally or nationally just because someone or other advises that it happen. Voters everywhere need to be re-educated. Voters everywhere need to be heartened. Voters need to begin to believe again that their vote can make a difference. There's a lot of cynicism out there. There's a lot of disillusionment out there. The task of re-engaging the voter in the political process is enormous. But it can be done.

In one local community, just outside of Pittsburgh, we tried to re-educate the voters by calling town meetings on issues very close to home.

[The town is McKees Rocks, Pennsylvania. Its politics is significant. Census data still gives evidence that the town has pockets of poor children and elderly, who are among the neediest in Allegheny County in the state of Pennsylvania. One can only wonder how Dole, in the light of the proposed medicaid and human service cut-backs, even dared to campaign for the presidency in McKees Rocks in July of '95 and face the poor about to get poorer if the cut-backs, proposed that year in Congress, happened. Also, one can only wonder how, since McKees Rocks, PA (not Ohio) is the hometown of Congressman John Kasich, he can claim not to know the deleterious effects that extreme human service budget-cutting and "State/County-controlled grants" have on a neighborhood's poor, given that he knows the present and past corrupt nature of the politics of his hometown.]

Both Dole and Kasich should consider the problems this town's poor faced in their struggle to overcome both their poverty and their corrupt local politics.

Shall we build a new high school, or simply add on to the one we have? Local school board officials had already decided, backroom style, to build a new high school, so the town meeting scheduled by a grassroots organization was a real threat to them.

Shall we create a neighborhood park four miles outside the neighborhood, or shall we put it in the center of town where the children would have easy access to it, and where it could serve as an after school community recreational and social center? The local Mayor had simply announced he had purchased land for the park four miles outside the town. It was a kickback deal made with a contractor friend.

Notwithstanding the "done deal" nature of these backroom decisions, the citizen-initiated town meetings were well attended. The voters came alive as they learned more about the issue, learned how it would affect their lives, and learned how they could bring about a new decision that would be in the best interests of the community.

At the town meetings, they quickly learned how to prioritize the tasks they needed to do. They began with phone calls, letter writing, getting other voters to attend the local council and township and school board meetings to address the issues, etc. And when all else failed, as inevitably it did, they organized and participated in a protest march around the government buildings and around the legislators' homes and places of business. Eventually, of course, the town's people hoped to vote most, if not all, the unsympathetic elected officials out of office. They did. [And there were even a few they sent to prison.]

Nothing does more for a voter than a local issue success. When the Mayor's decision was overturned, and it was decided by federal oversight administrators, pressured by the local voters, that the park was to be built in the center of the neighborhood where the children would have walking access to it, each voter stood tall in that moment of success. Their voice had made a difference.

Together, they had made a difference. They would try again. The local community voters were now energized in a way they had not experienced before. They were now feeling empowered. They were now feeling like employers. They were now aware that the public officials were their employees. They were now in charge, and they would remain in charge.

It was the beginning of a new day in one local community. Politics there will never be the same. Once corrupt, the local government is increasingly a more servant government. The voters democratized their local community.[29] It's a true success story. It did happen. Voters can make it happen elsewhere. Subsequently, in a memo he filed on the success of citizen empowerment in the town, Don Fisher, citizen leader wrote: "Stowe Township and McKees Rocks Boro are located just outside the city of Pittsburgh's southwestern limits, about five miles down the Ohio River from the Golden Triangle or from what is commonly known as the Pittsburgh Point where the three rivers, the Ohio, the Monongahela and the Allegheny, meet. The two communities are contiguous; both are equal in population with about 10,500 persons each. They form one neighborhood, with common transportation routes, shopping facilities, churches, a post office and a single school system for the children of both communities. They are old towns. They are working people's towns. Stowe is slightly younger and slighty more residential than McKees Rocks. Both are heavily industrial along the river bank and railroad lines, and become more residential in the surrounding hills and away from the river front. The business district is fairly active. The local business and governments of both are in deep financial trouble but are not flat on their face yet. The people of Sto-Rox are mostly white, from a wide variety of ethnic backgrounds. The black population is about 6% in McKees Rocks and about 1% in Stowe Township. There is a lot of people pride in the neighborhood. Basic Family structure is disintegrating, but it is happening more slowly than in most towns in spite of high unemployment, too many bars, and a general lack of recreational facilities. It is a poor place economically, but it is culturally rich and enriching.

Life is friendly and neighborly in Sto-Rox but enemy-lists grow, and suspicion mounts quickly when the topic of conversation turns to politics. There are complex inter-relationships. The groups whereby people organize themselves are their churches, clubs, boro, township, housing projects, County government employment, service organizations, etc. These units are all typically *status quo* and deeply entrenched in family allegiances that go way back.

In 1965 a simple question was raised and around that question a citizens meeting was called. The question was: Does McKees Rocks want to begin some programs under the Economic Opportunity Act, legislation administered by the federal Office of Economic Opportunity, and which was designed to initiate self-help programs in poverty-stricken neighborhoods? The citizens' response was typical enough in that the citizens wanted the program, and the assembled group was willing to serve as a fledgling citizen committee through which the federal funds would be received and administered. It was all standard procedure but the day's meeting was to have a strange and very unstandard ending.

The group just formed felt almost immediately stymied when they read in the legislation that they needed the Mayor's approval. Everyone was afraid to approach the McKees Rocks Mayor to ask for his cooperation. Seeking such cooperation (not necessarily permission or authorization) was a requirement in the procedures spelled out in the program's federal regulations." In his memo the citizen committee leader, Don Fisher, who was fairly new to the neighborhood subsequently wrote: "'When I asked why the fear?', the other members of the committee began to give me a short history course on McKees Rocks. I was told what I was soon to experience personally. Mayor David Hershman was not to be approached lightly. Most people stayed out of his way. Meetings of the sort that we were attending at the moment were not to take place without his approval, and because we were doing so, we were already in trouble. So the matter of approaching the Mayor was tabled for the moment, but we did decide to meet again and talk further. When at the second meeting of the citizen group, a local optometrist and I expressed some openness to visiting the Mayor, I suspected that we would be chosen as leaders of the group. We were. But I had no idea at the time that this was the beginning of a whole new movement that would forever change the public life of the people of Sto-Rox.

The following day as the designated leaders of the new citizen group, Dr. Horowitz and I [Don Fisher] went to the office of the Mayor. At the meeting with the Mayor, the Mayor's questions were clear: who are you? whom do you represent? what do you want? And finally, who in the hell do you think you are? His final statement, which abruptly ended the meeting, was equally clear and decisive: I play second fiddle to no one. This meeting is over.

The Mayor's questions were rhetorical. We had little chance to respond. It was clear he neither wanted or would listen to our response.

The Mayor of McKees Rocks had ruled the town like a king for over twenty-five years. He controlled countless jobs. He controlled the School Board. (McKees Rocks' schools merged with Stowe Township schools in 1966.) And he controlled the Boro Council. His patronage job control in Allegheny County was legendary. McKees Rocks had more citizens employed in County administration than any of the County's one hundred twenty-nine other Boroughs. Hershman also exercised almost total control of the votes of the residents of the three housing projects in Sto-Rox over which his brother was for many years his vote-controlling manager. The Mayor was to many whom we questioned, no further than their latest favor, a benevolent dictator. To those who felt his wrath, he was a ruthless tyrant. To be dismissed from his office usually meant just another reason to resent him. To be dismissed on that day in 1965 was different. When the incident was reported back to the other members of the citizen committee, these few people decided to fight rather than just to forget it. Their decision to struggle as a group against the Mayor, his patronage politics, and his autocratic control of everything from the local newspaper to the street cleaners was historic and was, I think, the beginning of a new Sto-Rox."

For at least a full year after this decision of the citizen committee, there was a battle for power and over which faction, the Mayor's or the citizen committee, would control and administer the federal poverty funds if they would come into town. During that year there were meetings, conferences, endless pickets, position papers, and almost daily meetings of the citizen committee members and its leaders. Appropriate resource persons were invited to these meetings as part of the effort to educate the citizenry regarding the issues.

The citizen group soon acquired notoriety in the state of Pennsylvania because of the intensity of the struggle, the infamy of the Mayor, and the appetite of the news media for good story.

At the end of that year the group was victorious. The citizen committee was designated by the H.U.D. office in Washington, D.C. to be the legitimate administrative arm of the anti-poverty program. The funds were to be sent directly to the group without interference by the Mayor or local Boro government. This was a major victory. It augured well for the integrity of the program. It would really be a program of service administered by the citizens, to and for each other.

As this political victory happened, an even greater breakthrough was happening in the hearts and minds of many people of the town. It was happening in the hearts of those struggling actively in the movement, and also in the hearts of those who timidly supported the movement from the sidelines.

There was a dramatic new awareness of new potential in the very wind that breezed over the town. We can do it! It is possible! It was the first time in anyone's experience that citizens had gathered together to do something that King David didn't like. It was the first time that citizens committed themselves to stay together until the issue was resolved.

There was a much quieter victory that happened in this year of conflict. Somewhere along the line in this developing self-help success story, the members of the citizen group decided to incorporate and stay together as a force for neighborhood improvement and for local liberty, no matter the pain and no matter the eventual outcome of the present conflict, no doubt the first of many yet to come.

During the following year of relative calm the newly incorporated group began to etch out its identity. The group now had status. It had a small office with expense money for its volunteer staff, and it had office equipment and supplies paid for with federal funds.

Significant advances in the struggle for local liberty occurred quietly as people began to learn how to look for the heart of the issues, how to put agendas together, how to conduct meetings, how to set priorities, etc. Initially, the group sponsored political awareness forums, raised money with bake sales and community concerts, initiated adult education and recreation programs, and in general took responsibility for the territory. One of the committee's most effective cultural and self-help achievements was the Nationality Festival which it organized, and which eventually drew about forty or fifty thousand visitors to the town every year. It was a real boon to the town's economy, and it helped to restore a sense of pride. The people began to sense they could speak about their town in a new way. Their town was no longer referred to by the media and others in the region as politically corrupt, oppressed and oppressive. It began to be described as a community on the move and on the way up.

Most of the controversy around the Citizen Committee and the poverty program centered in McKees Rocks. Stowe was involved by way of its being part of the McKees Rocks region. But Stowe's involvement grew deeper as the new poverty office began to serve the people of Stowe. It became even more involved, when the Citizen Committee, now incorporated, began to call the Sto-Rox School Board Administration to task for not including them in the planning of Title I federal programs, that were funded to enrich the lives of children with educational, nutritional, and physical handicaps. The Title I legislation required public hearings. None had been held by the Sto-Rox School Board.

When challenged by the Citizen Committee, the school officers were adamant. But the newly incorporated citizen group was not to be intimidated. The group became even more adamant. The citizens invited the appropriate state officials to review the issue. The investigation by the State resolved the problem in favor of the citizens and set a new local precedent for people participation in public school education's federal program decisions.

Soon after this victory, there was another dramatic crisis, maybe this time a very fortuitous one. It convinced grassroots folks that liberty is not easily won and not easily kept. It was the defining people empowerment moment in this neighborhood.

After a year of effectively administering the anti-poverty program, the citizen group hit another stone wall. The program so much needed in this neighborhood was now being opposed on the national level by congressional members, and was not to be refunded. Then came the Green Amendment, which as passed, essentially said that the anti-poverty programs nationally would not be dismantled all at once. Congressman Green's amendment proposed a compromise that would slow down the speed of the program's demise and allow for its future on a local level funding basis. Basically, the amendment said this: the local government has the right to determine whether or not the anti-poverty program will remain in the local community. It further suggested that local governments who so wished could in the next year retain and partially fund the programs [50%] simply because they were in place, and the benefits derived by the local residents were appreciable. Each subsequent year the federal funds would be diminished [by 50%] and the balance of the program costs would be absorbed by the local governments, and/or citizen-initiated self-sustaining fund-raising efforts.

The battle that then ensued in McKees Rocks was not about funds for the program. It was the power struggle, all over again. For by this time the anti-poverty program was almost self-sustaining. The required 50% match that would enable another year of federal funds to come into the community would be a match based on in-kind contributions. To continue the program would not cost the Boro a dime. In accord with the guidelines, the group could document its volunteer hours, put an in-kind dollar figure on them [It was well beyond the required 50% match.], and then submit that data in its proposal to H.U.D. for authorization to continue the anti-poverty program.

Notwithstanding, with utterly no concern for the good the service program had accomplished, King Mayor Hershman had his Council unanimously vote to end the program. The battle for power was on again.

For at least six more months after that vote of the Council, the struggle raged on, full force. But this time the people were more organized, more thoughtful in planning their strategy, and more dedicated than ever to keeping alive the new liberty they were experiencing. There was a more skillful use of the news media, and there were more carefully planned tactics to achieve their goals. During this phase of the struggle, for weeks and weeks, day after day, there was picketing of the Mayor and individual council person's homes in an effort to pressure the elected officials to change their vote.

In addition, many residents now boldly phoned the media and told about their personal experiences of oppression by the Mayor. Anyone who did so became infamous over night. Neighbors and relatives took distance from them. They became the enemy. It was difficult for many to stand up in their own neighborhood in this abrasive way for what they believed in. This was different than complaining about the evils of a federal and state government that was nameless, faceless, and far away. In this case in this local community, many alliances, friendships, and family relationships were put to the test as the issue became the talk of the town. This was a time when in the training sessions for the citizens, teachers hammered out the theme of what it is to take personal responsibility for justice and for the restoration of a new quality of life in the neighborhood, and where they stressed the need for commitment to the long term struggle.

It was invigorating to see the various groups in town struggling to change their attitudes toward the poor and oppressed. It was exciting to see people who had lost interest in politics years before begin to come politically alive again. It was perhaps most rewarding of all to see the people of the town losing their fear, speaking out, openly joining the movement, and regaining confidence in themselves. There were now many more people attending public meetings, and some were doing so for the first time in their sixty or seventy years of life in this community.

The camel's back was broken. It is still uncertain which straw did it. The pressure on every side was high. The break came when one of the most unlikely councilmen, after months of verbal abuse from him, changed his vote and stated his case in favor of the anti-poverty program continuing, and doing so under the administration of the citizen group. One by one the other council members followed.

A month after this breakthrough the Boro Council voted to dissociate themselves from the Mayor and to limit his powers. This was the first such action in twenty-five years on the part of a Council related to King David Hershman.

Not long after this vote, the anti-poverty program activities were humming along again. The Council and the citizens were together in the driver's seat and the Mayor, now a silent man at town meetings, was a man on his way out.

This scenario is what needs to play out across this nation. One local community after the other, one voter after the other, needs to feel the success that comes from making a difference in the local community's governing process. Once a voter makes a difference in the governing process, that voter is never the same thereafter.

Politically alive, the voter begins to see the connections. The voter begins to take charge of the process locally and begins to take new interest in the process nationally.

Politically alive, the voter will seek to know the way in which his or her congressional representative votes an issue. The voter will evaluate whether or not that vote is in the best interest of the most people nationally and locally, most of the time.

Politically alive, the voter will take charge of the election process. No more acceptance of campaign funds from what will then be policy - controlling interest groups.

Politically alive, the voter will see the need for campaign finance reform. The voter will know that only by and through publicly-funded campaigns will the elected officials be free to vote as their employers wish them to vote,- in the best interests of the people affected by the legislation.

Politically alive, voters will seriously begin to reform the system, removing one aberrant practice at a time.

Campaign financing, lobbying, and term limit reform are all part of one package. Both voters and the elected know we are caught in a web of our own making. The election and representational system is broken. The elected are not free to represent their constituents. The electors are not duly represented by those whom they elect. Both the elected and the electors are the losers.

WHO SPOKE WHAT MESSAGE IN ELECTION '94?

In the autumn of '94, the need for change was in the air. History will tell us that on November 8th of that year, the voters across the nation cast their votes and sounded their voices for change. To the surprise of even the most astute analysts and pollsters, the Republicans gained control of both the Senate and the House. The Republicans in the Senate gained eight seats, and with Democrat Shelby of Alabama crossing over, increased the Republican voting base to 53, compared with the Democrats' Senate voting base of 47.

The Republican Majority in the House gained fifty-three seats and now had a voting base of 230, compared with the House Democrats' voting base of 204. Moreover, no Republican incumbent lost their House or Senate seat. At this time also, 50% of the members of Congress would be in their first or second term, which means, as one analyst succinctly put it, "the old bulls are gone".[But were they?]

This much is certain. Power shifted. It happened. It is historical reality. But the why of it all is still up for grabs.

The interpretation of the November, 1994 vote remains with the interpreter. Many survivors, as well as astute politicians and observers of mid-term elections through the centuries, were now with guarded surprise in their voice asking, who spoke in this election and what was it they said? Many still wonder if the Republican victory was an unexpected fluke or the beginning of a deliberate trend. That question may be answered in the presidential elections of 2000.

Until then, the question remains unanswered. Who spoke in this election? Political historians will tell us that 38.7% of eligible voters across this nation voted. That's a little more than a third of the voters. They spoke.

The Republican victors believe that the 38.7%, who voted, spoke loudly and clearly in favor of the Contract With America principles framed by Newt Gingrich, the Speaker of the House. This Contract called for some pretty radical changes and included a promise of a vote on term limit legislation. It remains to be seen whether this was what 38.7% of the voters really wanted. But again, it's fact that the Republican Congress delivered on very little of its Contract with America in the 104th session. The few Bills successfully voted in the House never saw Senate action.

The Administration, meanwhile, claimed the November voters were saying, cut away the gridlock, negativity, and wasteful spending on the Hill, and get on with the business of governing.

The analysts were just puzzled by it all. This vote by 38.7% of the voters didn't seem to lend itself to any reasonably clear explanation, at least not yet.

And then what about the 62.2% of eligible voters who stayed home and didn't vote? Dare we conjecture what they were saying?

I can only theorize like the others. But I think that many of those voters who stayed home and didn't vote did so because they are just sick and tired of it all. In their homes and in their wallets, it doesn't make a bit of difference who is in power at the congressional level. Nothing really changes. Power, money, and the good life seem to stay with the wealthy who financially support the campaigns of the persons elected, and not with the middle class voters who, year in and year out, election after election, consistently do most of the voting, daily work hard at their jobs, and yet experience little change in their personal lives.

I also believe that many of the voters who stayed at home and did not vote were women, whose lives haven't been improved by the votes they have cast and the public officials they have supported. Perhaps they were just saying that as women, they are physically and psychically tired of it all.

They are tired of holding down a job, which they may no longer want but which is nevertheless essential to complement the salary of their partner, as together, they try to make due on the mortgage payments and the ever-increasing cost of living.

Women in today's world are working twice as hard as they did in the past when they were simply mothers and homemakers. Today, most women juggle two schedules. They are attempting to meet the demands of their offices and professional life as well as to satisfy the needs of their husbands and children.

They are wives, mothers, homemakers but they are also holding down a very competitive professional career. In most instances, they are working a seven day and night work week. They can't go back to the simple homemaker lifestyle. Yet many no longer wish to go forward on the level of activity at which they are held by the constraints of their dual life style, and by the glass ceiling for working women that still prevails in the workplace. Caught in this increasingly enigmatic quandary, I believe that women en masse chose not to vote in the November, 1994 mid-term election.

Many young voters between the ages 18 to 29 also chose not to vote in this election. Their excuse for not voting, in my opinion, probably ranged from forgetfulness to apathy, but the most resounding reason given to the pollsters was the lack of urgency in the issues the candidates were addressing. The campaign rhetoric was about medicare, welfare reform and tax cuts. These are just not issues young people think are worth fighting for, or worth believing in.

I also think racial and ethnic minorities did not vote in this election because they knew they were being voted against. Their self-interests were at risk. Proposition 187 on the West Coast dominated that region's elections, but extensive media coverage made Proposition 187 an issue in the consciousness of voters everywhere. Voters, especially minorities, saw that their personal suffering and cultural history was about to repeat itself in the lives of today's refugees and immigrants. They saw this proposition for what it was. To them it represented a tearing asunder of the very fabric of America and all that America stands for. "Give me your tired and your poor and your hopeless"; identify them as illegals, and I will deny them health care, education, and welfare services, no matter that they are aged or children. Or, as currently proposed by the legislators, even when you identify them as legals, I will deny them visas unless they are sponsored by a citizen (a wife, mother, or husband) who is earning more than 200% beyond the poverty level (about $38,000). Is this where we are heading as a government that claims to offer freedom, justice, and equal opportunity to all? I want no part of such an America, said many (minorities and friends of minorities) who would not vote for such a travesty of the democratic way of life.

Who then did cast the votes that put the Republicans into power. Some analysts, with whom I agree, are attributing the shift in power to the white male voters, an accident of the times in which today's middle class white male lives. In their vote some analysts seem to see a largely a-political message.

What was this message? What were today's middle class, white males saying?

The analysts tell us to look around and do a reality check. The average white male, the middle class white male, the forty to sixty thousand dollar salaried white male, has had it. He can't seem to make the American dream happen for himself and for his family. He works, and works, and has very little to show for it.

He sees his wife working. He tries to share the burden of homemaking and parenting that his working wife's schedule now makes necessary. Gone is the day when he would come home to a loving wife and a well-ordered home to enjoy a quiet dinner and a pleasant evening with his family.

More often than not, he and his wife arrive home at the same time. He may even come home first and when he does, he reads the notes from his wife that say, turn on the microwave and put the casserole in. And then. ... And then. ... And then. ...

And if that daily hassle isn't enough, when the end of the month comes, the bills are overwhelming. There's not very much left for the extras, much less for the contingencies, or vacations, or the retirement accounts. [All this, together with the downsizing trend and this decade's pervasive job insecurity, the middle-class American male isn't a happy camper.]

So what you have is very little financial gain, little family life, the daily hassle and juggling of schedules, anxiety about the future, less of the good life, and a gradual breakdown in the very fabric and identity of what makes the middle class white male who he once was, in contrast with who he now is.

There is just so much out of control in his home life and in his work situation. On the other hand, there seems to be so much that is corrupting, wasteful, and insensitive being done and undone by the elected officials. It is the stress and totality of all of this that is tearing away at the fabric of the American dream and the spirit of the American dreamer. There is this eroding of family life and this deterioration of wholesome neighborhoods, no longer free of crime and violence. There is the fast disappearance of the kind of economy that once assured that a man who worked hard all his life would be able to provide for his family. There is no longer the enduring self-assurance that he will be able to send his children to college.

Nor is there the assurance that he will be able to afford to vacation with his family, or to put aside savings for his retirement. This stress has to end. This subtle but constant eroding of self esteem has to stop.

So it is from out of the depths of this a-political ambiguity that I, too, believe with some of the analysts that the middle class white male voted in November of 1994.

Yes, the white male is employed. Yes, the white male looks prosperous. Yes, the white male seems to have it all. But behind the closed doors of his home and heart, the white male yearns for the days when a dollar bought a dollar's worth. The white male yearns for the day when he didn't work the first five months of a year to pay ever-higher taxes that yield little or no benefits. The white male yearns for the kind of life he knew when children grew up in homes where both parents were there to nurture, to inspire, and to evoke the best from their children and from each other.

FUNDING FOR MILLION DOLLAR CAMPAIGNS

Although a campaign finance reform bill was not among the list of bills the House Republicans promised America they would bring to a vote during the first one hundred days of the 104th Congress, the issue was very much on the front burner. But now it is no longer a hotly-debated issue although it is still often described as the test of resolve to change Washington.[30]

There are those proponents of campaign finance reform who say that money is corrupting the system and is the protector of privilege. Not too many would accept this somewhat naive blanket statement. Campaign financing is much more than that. It lies at the core of Washington's influence business.

Many debate whether the lobbyists and special interest contributors should be allowed to continue to give huge sums of private money to influence public policy. These huge sums are an affront to democracy.[31,32] On the other hand, given that campaigns in the future may be fully or partially financed with tax monies, it could be argued in reverse that taxpayers' dollars could put into office someone whom some taxpayers might seriously oppose.

Somewhere in-between these huge lobbying contributions and the taxpayers' dollars, there needs to be a campaign finance policy acceptable to most people most of the time. Individuals are now limited to no more than a $1,000 to any candidate for public office (President and Congress) per an election including primary, general, runoff, or special election, i.e., an individual can give $1,000 to a candidate for the primary, and $1,000 to the same candidate for the general election. An individual can also contribute to any political committee (DNC or RNC) of a national party the sum of $20,000, in the aggregate, per year and to any state PAC (Political Action Committee) the sum of $5,000 in the aggregate, per year. The maximum total political contribution that any individual can make during any calendar year is $25,000.

Corporations cannot directly give money to candidates or donate funds to a political campaign, but individual employees of a corporation can contribute their personal money to political candidates as defined above.

A general category called soft money is an exception to all the rules listed above. Soft money is money or in-kind contributions such as the use of company-owned hotel suites and conference rooms, given by individuals or corporations to state or national party-building foundations, or to non-profit groups that do much of the behind-the-scenes campaign scheduling. Soft money is subject to none of the usual federal disclosure rules and limits. Current campaign finance contribution limits were set down after the fiasco of the Nixon election campaign in late 1970. But the loopholes for corporate soft money

37

campaign financing are outside and beyond current legislation. Loophole campaign financing has no limits.

For example, although a corporation cannot give money directly to a candidate, it is not illegal to give huge sums to non-profit groups, who can then indirectly finance a candidate's bid (e.g. TV ads and live airtime) for election.

In other soft money loophole strategies, a corporation can give a no interest loan of a million or more to a group or an individual to help finance a specific campaign or campaign function.

Still another loophole that is legal is to give the candidate huge in-kind contributions such as allowing a candidate to plane-hop from state to state on the company-owned jet, etc.

Current campaign finance laws are woefully inadequate. The loopholes remain. No one foresaw that to get around the law that states that a candidate may only receive $1,000 from each contributor, campaigners and their parties set up Political Action Committees (PACs) in a wholesale fashion and in every state. There's no law that says this cannot be done. It's a legal nether world. No one ever thought that candidates would contribute or receive campaign financing funds from a PAC in any other but their own state.

As a result, a campaign funding system has developed whereby a candidate can receive contributions from multi-PACs. Any and all of these PACS can contribute to the campaigns of friends of the party across all state lines. This is now a widespread practice. Such interstate campaign financing then assures that a given party achieves or sustains a local, state or a national majority.

This practice is just shy of being illegal. But, nevertheless, it is legal. The perennial reform question is: how do we change the election laws in such a way that we keep the electorate engaged in the campaign financing process, and yet allow no one person or group to become a controlling interest.

There is still another dimension of the problem. Guidelines are needed that would not infringe on the First Amendment rights of any candidate, but that would set limits to the personal spending on the part of a candidate in a given campaign in an election cycle. Historically, the attempt to set such a limit was struck down by the Supreme Court in 1976. It was the Court's opinion then that such spending on the part of the candidate is protected by the constitutional right of free speech. But the issue is again with us. Voters looked askance at the twelve million dollars of personal money spent by wealthy Michael Huffington in a recent election campaign.[33] And then there was the twenty-five million that Steve Forbes indicated he was willing to spend during his run for the presidency. In less than two months in the '96 campaign, Forbes literally bought his way to the top tier of the presidential candidates. Relatively unknown in the first weeks of his campaign, he purchased ads that in some states ran every hour. As a direct result of that kind of unlimited spending power and TV exposure, the polls soon ranked Forbes second, Buchanan first, and Dole third in the race to be the Republican candidate for the presidency in 1996.

Currently in political history the greatest campaign expenditure for a candidate is the cost of television. Radio time and newspaper ads run a close second. One way to get at the problem of campaign finance reform is to level the media playing field. Media needs to be persuaded in the interests of the common good, to provide free or deep discounts on air time to each party's candidate, even as they already do, for example, in France where equal and no cost television time is allotted daily during the height of the campaign cycle to each major party candidate at the end of the regular evening news.[Thanks to Paul Taylor, a former Washington Post executive and now executive director of Free TV For Straight Talk Coalition, a proposal for free television time for presidential candidates surfaced in the U.S. in June of 1996. Several television networks made tentative offers. The Dole (financially strapped) campaign was quite enthusiastic about these free primetime TV offers. But the Clinton campaign, ahead in the polls and financially able, wasn't committing to what would be a drastic change in the electoral terrain at this time, and which could be construed as rewarding Dole for the over-spending he did to win his party's nomination in the primary elections.]

In future campaigns, in the interest of equal time and honest discussion of the issues, it is hoped that media will, not only offer free air time to the candidates, but may also limit even the volume of paid air time available to each candidate in an election cycle. That, of course, would be the best of all political worlds. It would require both integrity and philanthropy on the part of the media, who would then forego a measure of profit in order to restore more equitable competition to the campaign process.

Other related reform proposals are also under discussion. Some in Congress are considering a flat, federal-only tax credit to contributors, and then, only for in-one's own state contributions to political campaigns. Such a tax credit would put an end to the out-of-state campaign funding ostensibly designed to retain or obtain a party's majority in Congress. Such a carefully monitored and limited federal tax credit would also assure that both the rich and the middle class, the individual and the corporate sponsor, would have an opportunity to derive the same level of influence and tax relief from their campaign finance contributions.

Many other loopholes would be closed if full disclosure of campaign financing would be required, monitored, and credited on a federal-only level. One certainty is that it would more readily uncover the state to state aberrations when they do occur.

Another reform proposal suggested is to allow federal matching funds to be granted earlier in the campaign, and perhaps even granted quarterly, rather than annually.

There is even support surfacing for unlimited campaign funding but with full disclosure. Under this proposal a candidate, for example, may accept as much funding as offered from the tobacco or NRA lobby, but there would need to be full disclosure every step of the way. The candidate would need to be prepared for the media and voter criticism of the acceptance of such contributions particularly if the candidate's subsequent policy positions on tobacco and gun ownership issues shifted dramatically in favor of these contributors.

Notwithstanding any of these reform proposals, there is still the matter of personal wealth spending that seems to put wealthy candidates like Perot, Forbes, and Huffington above the law, no matter what future campaign financing laws might stipulate. (Inherent in this practice is the preclusion of otherwise able candidates, whose right to run for public office is rendered ineffectual for lack of funds to match the billionaires' run for the same office.) Parents can no longer tell their children that they may someday grow up to be President. Only parents who are billionaires can do so.

None of the proposed reforms covers the whole of the need for reform. None addresses all of the many dimensions of the problem or of the solution. None, for example, even touches on the reality that the current governance system as a system favors the incumbent.

Incumbents, for example, use the franking mailing privilege, to which the new candidates have no access. This privilege enables the incumbents to send campaign literature from their offices where as a matter of routine, their mailing costs are picked up by the taxpayers. In making use of this privilege, an incumbent can outspend and disadvantage the challenger running for office, who is paying for every stamp out of pocket.

There are hints of a reform proposal to deter the incumbent's ability to use this privilege in this way in the future. It has been suggested that a monetary figure be placed on the actual use of this privilege for campaign purposes, which in some instances is now valued at about a half million. The new candidates running for office would then be allowed to request and receive an equivalent matching funds amount over and above the present matching funds limit. If this occurred, it would somewhat level the campaign playing field.

To review these and other disparities in the campaign financing process, a bi-partisan Senate commission was proposed, and was endorsed by former Senator Dole, to draft recommendations to improve the campaign financing system in play. Nothing happened. The Commission never got off the ground.

In 1996 the Republicans were in power. They tried in the November election of 1996 to remain in power. Dole left the Senate to campaign throughout the remaining session of Congress for the office of the President. His initial nemesis within his own party was the unlimited spending power of candidate Forbes. It forced him to spend so much money on the primaries, he had little left to spend to complete his campaign in the general election.

The lack of campaign finance reform over the full length of his legislative career was something of Dole's undoing. By omission, he was caught in a net of his own making, - victim to the unlimited personal wealth of fellow Republican Forbes.

Another knotty issue in the net that caught Dole offguard was the disclosure in the media that scores of political donors, many of whom had millions of dollars riding on legislation, sidestepped the federal contribution limits by giving large sums of money to a political foundation chaired by Senator Dole. Candidate Dole was quick to announce that the donor list would be made public and that the foundation would be dissolved in the light of his presidential campaign. Foundation spokesman Hine also tried to minimize the fall-out by announcing that the foundation was set up in 1993 as a Republican think tank, and that Dole's legislative position in the Senate had nothing to do with contributions to the foundation.

Maybe so, but what we see here is evidence of the kind of legal loophole which allows special interest groups to deliver millions of dollars of so-called soft money to persons in politically powerful positions.

Something of the right words about needed campaign finance reform were spoken, perhaps again for the wrong reason, at the August 12, 1995 United We Stand America conference in Dallas. Representative Sam Brownback of Kansas stated at the conference that he was pushing a Bill that, "would eliminate the influence of political action or PAC committees, prohibit candidates for federal office from taking money from anyone outside their state, eliminate mass mailings in election years, and cut out all gifts, free trips and meals for members of Congress". To which Gingrich, also present at the conference, responded that such reform is needed "because our freedom is too important to let it be bought off in a wave of money from a variety of sources that we don't understand and can't even follow".[34] The right words spoken but, again, little action followed this rhetoric.

Another serious soft money issue that needs attention is the practice of exempting in the name of deregulation, industry's campaign contributors from the burden and cost of compliance with federal regulations. Pork barrel projects was once the name of the game. Now the pressure is on the legislators to deregulate and to allow industry whatever it takes to increase corporate profits. They do this by enacting legislation and formulating administrative measures that eliminate many of the environmental, safety and labor provisions that industry formerly had to meet.[35] Strange as it seems, this relationship between legislation and an industry's campaign finance contribution to the legislator is no longer hidden. House and Senate staffers know that legislative action hinges on the size and extent of campaign contributions.[36] Staffers go through the motions but they realize the provisions of a bill are decided long before a piece of legislation comes to a floor vote. In each such instance both the consumers and the voters lose; former and current legislators also lose.

A case in point was that of Sun Diamond Growers, an agricultural cooperative, which had been charged with trying to illegally influence the decisions of Mr. Espy, Secretary of Agriculture. Both denied any wrongdoing. But the appearance of something amiss was there.

Situations like these are very troubling to those of us who keep hoping for system reforms that are long overdue.[37]

Among the voices for reform is that of Colin Powell.[38] "It's a little shocking to see how quickly freshman congressmen are spending a great deal of their time raising money. Why do all these corporations pour a ton of money into helping some guy from a district somewhere in Oregon prepare himself for the next election? The answer is they are buying affirmative action; they are buying preference; they are buying quotas. ... all the things we think are terrible when the same terms are applied to minorities and those of our citizens we think are less advantaged." It's clear that Powell knows and sees the connections between wealth and influence. But where's the action?

What will it take? How much worse must it get before true reform will be legislated? How much more evidence do we need that legislation and public policy is fast becoming heavy-handed and heavy on the backs of the poor, even while the rich prosper? What will it take to convince both legislators and voters that this is what happens when public policy is the result of "too many dollars; too little sense"?

Just after the Senator Packwood disclosures, Washington was very concerned about excerpts from the former Senator's diary that described his monetary arrangements with lobbying firms.

Then came the emergence of single-member lobbyists like Ann Eppard, who rose from the position of administrative assistant to the role of a lobbyist of stature when her former employer Bud Shuster was appointed to chair the Transportation and Infrastructure Committee, one of the most powerful committees in this Congress.[39]

That reality, together with Perot's threat of a third Party, with six of its nine platform planks calling for steps to rid the political system of special interest money and influence,[40] impelled Senators McCain (S.1219) and Feingold (S.46) in June of 1996 to produce campaign finance reform Bills that would have legislated subsidies for low-cost mail and television advertising to candidates who would abide by "voluntary" spending limits. The problem with this Senate reform effort (in addition to its hidden public financing), was that this reform legislation came too late in a presidential election year and congressional session - that was already extremely partisan. The legislation never got past the cloture vote.

The House leadership made its own last minute campaign finance reform effort. But the House Bill proposed by Linda Smith of the state of Washington (H.R.2566), and an alternative proposed by Bill Thomas of California (H.R. 3820) were also defeated 259 to 162, and 243 to 177, respectively.

When reform does come, hopefully it won't be as inane as it was in the state of Kentucky. In Kentucky a new campaign finance law was tested as the election for the governor in 1996 got underway. Both parties subsequently admitted its flaws. It was the right thing to do, but the reform led to the wrong side effects. The new law sharply limited political contributions and spending. As a result both candidates lacked the funds to travel, to hire staff, or to run the television ads that for many voters represented a principal source of political information. So the election in Kentucky that year was less corrupt, but the interest of the voters was seriously diminished.[41]

Notwithstanding, something of an increasingly popular trend to call for campaign finance reform is on the horizon on the Hill these days.[42] Now that it's getting too hot for many legislators in the kitchen of budget and regulatory reform, they are turning to campaign reform as a relatively harmless re-election ploy. Voters might be well advised that in the near future as the 2004 elections draw near, if it looks like a duck and it walks like a duck and talks like a duck, it may not be a duck. It's once again, an empty promise.

Last time round, (and we can bet he will do it again in the year 2004 election cycle), candidate Buchanan proposed a broad political reform program, he didn't leave out much that is wrong with the system, and all of which has at one time or another had its moment in the sun. He urged legislation that would allow states to impose term limits on lawmakers. He proposed banning congressional pensions. He said members of Congress should not be allowed to accept gifts worth more than fifty dollars from a single source. He proposed that contributions to House and Senate candidates be limited to one thousand dollars a person for primaries and general elections. He proposed that House candidates not be allowed to accept campaign finance contributions from outside their district, and Senate candidates from outside their state.[43]

It's evident that like his colleagues then and now, he knows what's wrong with the system. The system is broke and the system needs fixing.

But I'm convinced that the fixing will only come when informed voters evaluate, not the rhetoric, but the performance of their employees, the legislators, each time they cast a vote. Voters need to begin to vote from out of the conviction that as a nation, we experience less and less democracy when too many dollars and too little sense give us legislation, that is pre-paid for.

At this moment in history the political heart of this great nation is sick. The political heart of this nation cries out for comprehensive reform of the political system.

Who will be president in the year 2001 is now known. It is Mr. Bush. But history will record that the presidential campaign and the legislative sessions which immediately preceded it, whatever else it did, it clearly brought to light the ills and reform needs of this century's election process.

Follow the money trail is that bit of ancient wisdom that can still explain why government is simply not working for ordinary folks. Too many "veteran" elected officials have a price. Wealthy special interests pay that price and buy influence. These same wealthy special interests then exploit the loopholes in current tax laws and in far too many instances pay little or no taxes on huge profits. The rest of us are left with the tax burdens inflicted on us by the legislators and the lobbyists.

In 1996 the first Tax Free Day was May 10th. On this day in that year, the media rather glibly announced that each of us worked the first three hours of every day in the first five months of the year, to pay our taxes.

It seems pretty clear that tax reform and campaign finance reform are inter-related. But it's equally clear that neither is a priority issue on the agenda of the Congress, now or in the immediate future.

So reform proposals over the years have come and gone. Few believe that serious campaign finance reform will reach passage in this 106th Congress. We remember that Gingrich promised debate and a vote in late fall of 1995, or early Spring of 1996 on campaign finance reform, but nothing happened.

In the Senate, in June of 1996, the McCain S. 1219, did reach the Senate floor. This Bill would have encouraged Senate candidates to accept voluntary campaign-spending limits in exchange for subsidized tv time and reduced postage rates. The Bill would also have barred state PAC committee contributions to federal candidates. But the Bill never got beyond cloture. Again, nothing happened.

In this presidential election 2000 year, Senator McCain campaigned for the presidency on the issue of campaign finance "soft money" reform. Though initially successful, his campaign hit rock bottom. Now Gore and Bush call themselves "reformers" as they vie for the presidency. Presidential candidate Al Gore & his Vice President nominee, Senator Joseph Lieberman, promise that campaign finance reform will be the first bill introduced in 2001 in their administration, if and when they are elected to office. But they were not elected.

REFORM PROMISES, PROMISES, PROMISES

Are we today in the embryonic stages of another Boston tea party revolution? Voters increasingly know that their vote is meaningless and they know, too, that on most issues before the Congress, they are without true representation. They also know that career politicians are too powerful to be tolerated any longer by the voters. Power corrupts. The more absolute the power becomes, the more corrupt is the use of the power. This is not just a cliché. It is fact. One only has to look around and about this nation to see that there is a growing discrepancy between those who have and those who have not; between those who have, want, and get more, and those who have not and are the most vulnerable to have even less.

What the voters want from the Congress in this new century is institutional reform that will give them the assurance that the performance of their legislators is representative of and more aligned with the real needs of the electorates who employ them.

We already know that little action on campaign finance reform happened in preceding sessions of Congress.

Political historians will remember though that on a Sunday in New Hampshire on June 11, 1995, President Clinton and House Speaker Gingrich shook hands before the television cameras and promised America that they would work together and create a commission to bring about campaign finance reform. This pledge met with one setback after another. In the week that followed the handshake, President Clinton wrote a letter to Gingrich outlining a way to structure the proposed commission for campaign finance reform. [Shortly thereafter, the President phoned Frank MacConnell Jr. of Claremont, New Hampshire to personally reaffirm his commitment to implement Frank's idea to create a type of non-partisan commission, like a [military] base closure commission, to review the campaign finance system.]

Gingrich responded in a television interview that he was upset that the President had laid out the structure for the commission for campaign finance reform without consulting him. He questioned whether the whole idea was just another political gimmick, even as he claimed he needed more time to study the effect of money on politics. [He will probably in the years to come author a million dollar book or two on the subject. This promise, like his others, went nowhere. No commission was formed; the issue of campaign finance reform remained at a standstill.}

Subsequently, Clinton's own stance on campaign finance reform was muddied when the Democratic National Committee put out a memo which advised that those who contributed a hundred thousand dollars to his re-election campaign would have dinner with the President. Those who contributed $50,000 would have dinner with the Vice President. And those who contributed a $1,000.00 would have lunch with the First Lady. To most people this didn't sound like reform. It was the same old jargon. However, when the President heard about this memo, he was furious and ordered the Democratic National Committee to withdraw the offer. But the damage was already done. It dimmed the clarity of the Clinton promise of campaign finance reform. Moreover, this promise was not kept.

Campaign financing explains why reform is needed in many of the departments and agencies of government. Legislators "bought and paid for" are not free to legislate for needed reform. Nevertheless, reform does not mean throwing out the baby with the bath water. Reform does not mean abandoning a sense of history and ignoring the wisdom and rule already achieved through due process and collective experience. The United States has its fair share of corruption and injustice; it has its victims of both. But the United States as a nation is strong and decent; its public policies and budget priorities are such that its citizens can stand proud and tall in this or in any other country in the world. Congressional legislation and budget appropriations need to continue to assure a better future for all, and can never be allowed to favor the wealthy while disfavoring society's most vulnerable.

The voters of this country know what happened under the Republican-led Congress of 1996. While the middle class was strategically distracted with counting their fool's gold of a few hundred dollars per child tax credit, the corporate wealthy were banking the real gold they amassed when industrial safety and environmental deregulation set in, when healthy competition disappeared, and when fair play in business and the trades was no longer subject to standards, consumer safeguards, or guidelines of any significance. On June 26, 1996, D.C.'s major newspaper editorialized this state of political affairs and described it this way: "What is excessive in [today's] politics is not the [campaign finance] money spent, but the amount of political power that government in our time has to direct economic outcomes and regulate behavior. ... Congress can either put whole industries at risk or hand them a subsidized bonanza,...."[44]

Perhaps the campaign reform proposal by Larry J. Sabato and Glenn R. Simpson, and discussed in "Dirty Little Secrets: The Persistence of Corruption in American Politics", may be an idea whose time has come. These authors advocate "no limits on how much a candidate can receive or spend", but they call for full disclosure and strict enforcement by heavy fines on an industry when their profits are directly related to their campaign contributions. It's what might be called the stock market principle for campaign finance reform.

These authors suggest that a well-informed marketplace [where huge profits cannot be hidden and do not go unnoticed], rather than [government] bureaucrats [or even well-informed voters], should be the judge of whether a legislator has accepted too much money from a particular interest group, or an industry has profited unduly from a contribution to a particular legislator.

I would like to add to this proposal. I suggest that the fines collected, which I believe would be in the billions, ought to be used to benefit single mothers, the elderly and the middle class. Otherwise, in the present governance context, the most vulnerable in today's world will simply get poorer even as they will get less in the way of school lunches, nutrition supplements, job education and health care.

I also say this because for Congress, good reform ideas seem hard to come by. In 1996, the reform idea, for example, of giving Block Grants to state and local governments for welfare, nutrition, and health care programs was one of their bad ideas. It's bad because when the money runs out, the food and health care needs will simply go unmet. No more money, no more human services.

Having spent or mispent the capped Block Grant, a State will not be able to appeal to the federal government for more monies to meet the growing needs of the poor in their particular state. Either they will raise state taxes to do so, or the poor of their state will go hungry and be without health care. Worse case scenario, the poor in their state will migrate to a near or distant state that is willing to spend state tax dollars for the benefit of those in need.

Also, when other government needs are pressing, the already seriously limited human service monies will simply be diverted by the state and local governments and used for emergency budget items such as a new fire truck, a broken sewer line, and whatever.

There's a third reason that the Human Service Block Grant to the states was a bad idea. Most folks won't talk about it. However the other day on Channel Five, a gray-haired staffer in Senator Moynihan's office had the courage to say on national television that Block Grants are a bad idea because the first forty percent or more of the funds will go to the mob world.

From experience I know there's a lot of truth in this even if we first concede that every elected official is good, well meaning, and honest.

The Block Grants to each State are passed from the Governor down to the County and then to the local government units. At each stage there are upfront administrative costs, and then there are the hidden kick-backs. When, for example, I administered a Block Grant for meals for the elderly in McKees Rocks Boro in Allegheny County in the state of Pennsylvania, no matter how inadequate and mish-mash the food delivered was, and no matter how as administrators we complained, we had no leverage in the matter. We could only contract for meals with the County's choice of a caterer. No one had to tell us why. I for one continue to believe, that the mob-connected catering service we had to use, kick-backed to the County and to the Boro. And that meant less monies for quality menus, and little or no quality control of the food served to the elderly.

It seems remnants of this practice are still to be found. In D.C. recently, the administrator of the District's school lunch program resigned because she was told that she could only contract for meals for the children from a designated contractor even though she knew that these meals as delivered were of poor quality. Subsequently when her outcry hit the media, the School Board terminated the food contract and "reviewed" the situation.

Sadly enough, we've gone down the Human Services Block Grants to state and local governments before. It is not a reform measure. Federal standards, federal monitoring, and federal administration of block grant programs should never be abandoned in the name of reform. Creative and uniquely-tailored State implementation, yes. Without any federal safeguards, no.

So even as we were pseudo-reformed by the 1996 Congress going down this road again, the influence of the lobbyists and newly-created single issue pressure groups has grown stronger. Lobbyists pressure for less federal controls and for more deregulation. They pressure, in the name of corporate profits, for a return to legislation that will bring us back to square one on many of the issues, particularly the environmental and the food safety issues, - battles that we fought and won in the past.[45,46]

In a brilliant but costly political move, President Clinton in June of 1995, presented a balanced budget to the Congress and to the American people. The Congress objected to this initial FY '96 budget because it wasn't scored, so they said, by the Congressional Budget Office. [They objected as well to a second balanced budget that Clinton presented in December, 1996 and that was scored by the CBO.] Their objections had little to do with scoring by the CBO. Congress objected because it took the steam out of their own call for a balanced budget,and exposed for all to see that their budget proposal was in reality designed to cut human services and education spending in favor of a tax cut for the wealthy, and hidden profits for industry.

To present a balanced budget scored by the CBO, as he did in 1996, was a way for the President as leader of this nation to get back into the budget process and hold the congressional leaders accountable to the people. Presenting his balanced budget (s) was a way for the President to tell the American people that it was just not dollars and human service programs that Congress was cutting from the budget.

What was being cut out of the budget in 1996, supposedly to reduce and eventually eliminate the deficit, was long-standing public policy that defines education,job-training, health care, environmental reforms, and concern for children and the elderly as this nation's public policy priorities.

History will yet prove or disprove the effect of the President's budget leadership gesture in 1996 in behalf of the common good and as a way to sustain sound public policy priorities. I believe it was a defining gesture by this President to move this country forward into a new age of non-partisan legislating, such as would restore true and balanced democratic principles to public policy, budget priorities, and budget appropriations.

Historians will one day record the effects on future generations which this 1996 legislative moment has had. Although gridlock and negativity in the legislative process still seems to prevail, this 1996 moment in political history brought the need for non-partisan governance into greater focus. Voters everywhere were then as now rightfully concerned with the lack of civility and downright aggression between members of the two parties. Left unchecked, this could lead to implosion of the political system.

Voters in 1996 were genuinely upset with the extreme reforms Congress was proposing. The deregulatory reforms were creating a field day for industry and corporations who were making billions even as they spent a mere million or two paying accountants to do the risk assessments and cost analyses the deregulatory reform process required.

Meanwhile, the major concern of the rest of us is that once again, we are asked to bear the impact that all of this radical deregulation of long-standing and safe and secure practices is having on the environment, on the water we drink, on the food we purchase at the markets and that we eat at our tables. (Not too long ago, headlines were filled with the effects of the mad cow disease in Great Britain, - prime example of where questionable reform deregulation may lead us.)

And our second, and equally grave concern is that Congress too often is legislating, not according to the will and the interests of the voters, but is legislating in accord with the will of the wealthy lobbyists, who lobby for ever-greater profits for industry and who are camped on the congressional doorstep.

We are at a moment in the political history of this country when legislation and public policy are no longer created by, for, and of the people. To the contrary, legislation and public policy are fast becoming undemocratic. Legislators are increasingly less representative of their constituents.

We are faced with a watershed moment in voter response. Voters today need to evaluate and reject what is happening in their homes and in this nation when legislators and legislation are so blatantly influenced by too many dollars and too little sense.

Paulette G. Honeygosky

VOTERS ARE CYNICAL

Voters are watching the political charades in Congress more closely than they are given credit for. Voters are cynical but voters are poised to act. A National Movement To Restore The Rights Of The Electors And The Rights Of The Elected is long overdue. The task of reform rests with both the elected and the electors.

Campaign finance and election reform legislation will come. But the reform of the electoral system ultimately begins and ends with the electors. In the first instance, voters need to vote into office qualified candidates. Voters need to monitor the performance of the elected. Only well informed voters can evaluate, direct and pressure their legislators to do what is best for the common good. If all else fails, the voters can vote the bums out of office.

On the other hand, the elected need to legislate for comprehensive reform of the political process that undergirds the democratic way of life.

The elected need to vote each issue in terms of the interests and needs of their constituents.

The elected need to know when their effectiveness is over and return voluntarily to their homes and careers, encouraging new blood and persons with new ideas to replace them. Term limits or limits on committee chairmanships would become unnecesssary. Congressional pensions could be limited to no more than twelve years. And voters could otherwise vote out those who were ineffective and stayed in office too long.

All gifts to elected officials would be taboo. No exceptions. When not to accept a gift would insult the giver, the gift could be passed on to a state museum or (if edible or monetary) passed on to a non-profit group that serves the needy.

Campaign finance reform legislation should be comprehensive, not piecemeal. Partial or total or no funding at both the State and Federal level by the taxpayer should be debated and uniformly implemented across the nation.

Corporate funding could be grounded in what has been called, the stock market principle, that would allow unlimited campaign contributions but would demand full disclosure of both profits and campaign contributions. The marketplace would then monitor itself. Hidden contributions or undue profits based on contributions that buy policy shifts (or deregulation) would be disclosed by the market itself and heavy fines would be imposed.

Maximum individual contributions annually could remain, as currently legislated, at $25,000.

Pork barrel spending tacked onto legislative Bills is out.

By current law, as of February 1996, all lobbyists are to register with the Clerks of the Senate and the House respectively. The semi-annual lobbyists' disclosure forms should more clearly spell out who the lobbyist visits on the Hill, and whether or not radical policy shifts then ensue. Fines should be levied when disclosure is found wanting, or when legislation is discovered to be pre-paid for.

Free and fair access to the process and to the legislator is imperative. No special I.D.s or open Capitol Hill door policies for lobbyists. No pre-paid-for seating for lobbyists at public hearings.

No interstate PAC funding for incumbents or challengers. To that end, the names of all candidates who receive PAC funding at the State level would need to be clearly disclosed to the Federal Election Commission, together with the names of all who contribute to PAC's within the State.

No (in kind) soft money loopholes. All in-kind contributions, by legislative mandate, would be given a monetary value and disclosed on appropriate reports.

All individual or corporate contributions would be filed with the IRS and only a federal tax credit allowed. No State tax deductions would be granted.

The FCC could encourage that a percentage of no-cost tv coverage be given to each candidate. The total coverage, paid or free, and allowed each candidate could be limited.

Postage costs covered by the franking privilege and enjoyed by the incumbents would need to be offset by subsidized or low-cost postage for all other candidates.

Other abuses against the Electors and the Elected could be written into reform legislation upon hearing the testimony of those public officials who over the past decade have been convicted by the courts of white collar crimes against the electorate.

In presidential campaigns federal matching funds allowed under present or future law could be granted quarterly, not annually.

A spending limit for total campaign spending should be set. (This year the campaigns for the presidency will cost an estimated $1.5 billion. Last election cycle, Michael Huffington's Senatorial campaign cost $44 million.) Free speech, yes. But the Constitution gives no one the right to buy an election, or to destroy the reputation of a less wealthy candidate. Healthy competition needs to be restored to the electoral process.

The current presidential election campaign has reached an all time low in sleaziness. Bush or Gore ought to heed the message of the times. Governance that will take us into 2001 needs to be round-tabled. Power can never again be absolutely held by any one party. Power is to be shared. The pyramid of political power needs to be configured in such a way that the elected and electors, the Republicans, Democrats and the Independents, can begin to feel again that they are co-participants, no one of whom is expendable.

The twenty-first century deserves better. It demands wisdom of the heart from both the elected and the electors. It invites greatness. It requires a President and citizenry with vision, compassion, humility, and competence to take this nation into an age of participatory governance. I look forward to such a future even as did, Wilfrid Desan who brilliantly wrote recently, "Let [such a] The Future Come". Let such a presidency and such a citizenry come. Let true governance by and for all the people, not just for the lobbyists and their campaign-financing employers, be with us once more.

Mr. President, abolish soft money. Allow the elected and the electorate to experience democracy at its best! Put an end, once and for all, to the way campaigning for election to public office is: - Too Many Dollars; Too Little Sense.

Postscript

_____It's the year 2001 and the soft money scandal grows. A recent Common Cause report indicates that the soft money system of funding campaigns has grown from $86 million in 1992 to $262 million in 1996; the statistics are not yet in for the Bush vs Gore Campaign 2000, but voters know it is already well into the billions.

Presidential candidates Senator John McCain, a Republican, and former Senator Bill Bradley, a Democrat, made history in December,1999 with a handshake that made campaign finance reform the centerpiece of their presidential primary campaigns. History will record that both lost their bids to become the candidate chosen by their respective parties, but history will also record that their pledge, their historic handshake on the issue, has helped create the climate for campaign finance reform that will and must come.

McCain ironically was defeated when a group called Republicans for Clean Air suddenly surfaced - just before the New York and California primaries and pumped $2.5 million into television ads attacking him, The "group" turned out to be two Texas brothers, Charles and Sam Wyly, who have been identified as major donors to Gov. George W. Bush. C'est la vie!

Too little, too late, - just after McCain's defeat in the primaries, - the House and Senate passed legislation that now requires tax-exempt groups, "the so-called 527 groups" that secretly raise and spend money on elections, to disclose their activities. One very tiny step toward campaign finance reform. (In its original Senate form, the author of this measure was Senator Joseph Leiberman, the Democratic nominee for the office of Vice President.)

But even as this tiny win occurred, term limits has again surfaced as an issue worth watching. In States where term limits were passed and promises were made by candidates in 1990, their promises have now come due. To keep their promises, they should step down. Yet they are running - some for their fourth terms in the House (though they promised not beyond six years) and for their third term in the Senate (though they promised not beyond twelve years).

All of the above leaves us with the promise - that whoever (and we now know it is Bush and Chaney) is elected to the office of President and Vice President respectively, - Campaign Finance Reform will be the first bill introduced and passed in their administration. Will this promise be kept? That, my fellow Americans, is the question before us.

Footnotes

1 "Congress Re-Entrenches", Editorial, The Wall Street Journal, January 25, 1994
2 "Capitol Hill Support For Curbs On Lobbying Masks", John Harwood, The Wall Street Journal, April 20, 1994
3 "What About Reform For Congress", Editorial, The Washington Post, January 26, 1994
4 "The First Train Wreck", Editorial, The Wall Street Journal, September 21, 1995
5 "Nan Cries Foul", Editorial, The Wall Street Journal, October 5, 1995
6 "The Real Welfare Debate", Editorial, The Wall Street Journal, September 18, 1995
7 "Demeaning Opposition to Welfare Reform", Editorial, The Wall Street Journal, September 26, 1995
8 "How The Biggest Lobby Grew", Lindley H. Clark, Jr., The Wall Street Journal, January 17, 1994
9 "Ports Employ Varied Tactics To Curry Washington Favor," William L. Roberts, The Journal of Commerce, October 3, 1994
10 "Former Lawmaker [Glenn English] Says Lucrative Job As Lobbyist Offered Way Out of Congress", John Harwood, The Wall Street Journal, January 24, 1994
11 "For The Baby Bells, Government Lobbying Is Hardly Child's Play", Rick Wartzman & John Harwood, The Wall Street Journal, March 15, 1994
12 "Coelho On Congressional Reform", Albert R. Hunt, The Wall Street Journal, February 3, 1994
13 "Term Limits Not So Fast", The Economist, February 19, 1994
14 Letter to the Editor, Rep. Bill McCollum, The Wall Street Journal, March 8, 1995
15 "Honor Thy Contract", Editorial, The Wall Street Journal, February 10, 1995
16 "Voters Be Dammed", Editorial, The Wall Street Journal, August 24, 1994
17 Congressional Record, H3929, March 29, 1995
18 "You Didn't Mean That Term Limit Stuff, Did You?, Paul Gigot, The Wall Street Journal, March 10, 1995
19 Congressional Record, H3928, March 29, 1995
20 "The Term Limits Scam", Editorial, The Washington Post, March 12, 1995
21 The Wall Street Journal, March 9, 1995
22 "Voters to House: Six Years & Out", Edward H. Crane, The Wall Street Journal, February 17, 1994
23 "No Uncertain Terms", Editorial, The Wall Street Journal, November 29, 1994

24 Evans-Novak Political Report, November 29, 1994
25 "Voters In Several States, D.C. Heavily Favor Term Limits", Dana Priest & William Claiborne, The Washington Post, November 9, 1994
26 "Even With New GOP Majorities In Both Houses, Term Limits Face Likely Doom In Congress", Jackie Calmes, The Wall Street Journal, November 28, 1994
27 "Speaking of Term Limits", Editorial, The Wall Street Journal, November 4, 1994
28 "To House Democrats: Get A Minority Mindset", Editorial, The Wall Street Journal, November 17, 1994
29 Neighborhoods Can Transform, Paulette Honeygosky, 1990
30 "Campaign Finance Reform May Prove The Test Of Republican Resolve To Change Washington", Rick Wartzman, The Wall Street Journal, November 18, 1994
31 "Money - Still The Mother's Milk of Politics", Mickey Edwards, The Wall Street Journal, November 8, 1994
32 "Some Of Washington's Influence Peddlers Reap Added Benefit Of Stake In Firms They Promote", Jill Abramson & David Rogers, The Wall Street Journal, November 11, 1994
33 "Requiem For 'Reform'", Editorial, The Wall Street Journal, October 15, 1994
34 "Reps Smith, Brownback Seek Help From Perot Group For Campaign Reformw", Editorial, Bureau of National Affairs, Inc., August 15, 1995
35 "Budget-Cutting Republicans Repackage Pork As Regulatory Relief For Their Business Allies", David Rogers, The Wall Street Journal, August 22, 1995
36 "The Best Congress Money Can Buy", Albert R. Hunt, The Wall Street Journal, September 7, 1995
37 "Eppard's Clients Win Some, Lose Some", William L. Roberts, The Journal of Commerce, February 8, 1996
38 "Colin Powell Able To Speak His Mind, Criticizes Conservatives, Businesses", Gerald F. Seib, The Wall Street Journal, September 18, 1995
39 "Emergence Of Single-Member Lobbying Raises Fresh Concerns In Post-Packwood Washington", Jill Abramson, The Wall Street Journal, March 8, 1995
40 "McCain Throws Reform Lifeline To Needy GOP", Gerald F. Seib, The Wall Street Journal, February 10, 1995
41 "Kentucky's New Campaign - Finance Law Limits Donations As Well As Interest In Governor's Race", John Harwood, The Wall Street Journal, March 23, 1995
42 "Campaign Finance - Deformed, Bradley A. Smith, The Wall Street Journal, November 29, 1994

43 "Buchanaan Proposes Broad Political Reform Program", Tim Shorrock, Evans-Novak Political Report, November 29, 1994
44 The Washington Post, April 21, 1996
45 "The GOP's War On Nature", Editorial, The New York Times, May 31, 1995
46 "New Single-Issue Pressure Groups Sprout Up On The Right To Support The Republican Agenda", The New York Times, May 31, 1995

Appendix I

H 3884 - H 3965
CONGRESSIONAL RECORD - HOUSE March 29, 1995

TERM LIMITS HISTORIC DEBATE EXCERPTS AND VOTE IN THE HOUSE

(Mr. DeFAZIO [Democrat from Springfield, Oregon] asked and was given permission to address the House for one minute and to revise and extend his remarks.)

Mr. DeFAZIO. Mr. Speaker, Speaker GINGRICH's whip organization has been awesome as he has rolled up victory after victory no matter how controversial his legislative agenda.

He rolled up a large majority of Republicans to push GATT through a lame duck Congress. Speaker GINGRICH did yeoman's work behind the scenes to deter any congressional scrutiny of the $40 billion Mexico bailout, and when we finally forced a vote on the floor the Republican leader threatened committee assignments, subcommittee chairs and other retaliations if his minions did not toe the line.

Just last week they flexed their leadership muscle gain on welfare and nutrition reform, but the muscles of the Speaker's whip organization have suddenly gone flaccid with the prospect of term limits.

AMERICA NEEDS TERM LIMITS

(Mr. Fox of Pennsylvania asked and was given permission to address the House for one minute and to revise and extend his remarks.)

Mr. FOX of Pennsylvania. Mr. Speaker, we need to adopt term limits. Eighty-five percent of the American people support limits on the time a Member may serve in Congress.

The current system of entrenched power and almost perpetual incumbency has produced a political climate of cynicism and distrust among the American people. Term limits, with their built-in mandate for accountability, can move us toward restoring faith of a wary public in their government in Washington.

Mr. Speaker, this is not a partisan issue. While Republicans just won control of both Houses for the first time in 40 years, we are reaching across the aisle and urging our Democrat colleagues to join us in fundamentally changing the way

Washington works. It is my hope that the voters' demand for change will not become just another electoral echo but will remain vivid and distinct in our ears.

The American people deserve a Congress that is answerable directly to them. This is the meaning of the 1994 election. Mr. Speaker, we want a Congress that is truly a reformed Congress; that demands term limits now.

TO THE DEMOCRATS: JOIN US

(MR. LAHOOD asked and was given permission to address the House for 1 minute.)

MR. LAHOOD. Mr. Speaker, where are the Democrats? We need you. We need you today.

It takes 290 votes. Twenty-two States, many of the States that you all come from, have passed term limits. Why do you not get the message?

Many of these people are Democrats in these 22 States. They need for you to come to the floor today and support the vast majority of Republicans that will vote for term limits.

Do not snub your nose at your people. Come and join us. Help us put the 290 on the board and give the people of the country a chance, an opportunity to debate term limits so it will go out to every State legislature, so all the people will have a chance to debate it.

Do not snub your nose at the voters. Give them a chance to have a say in this. Come and join us. Put the 290 on the board today. Join us.

CONGRESSIONAL TERM LIMITS

(Mr. ROEMER asked and was given permission to address the House for 1 minute and to revise and extend his remarks.)

Mr. ROEMER. Mr. Speaker, I have to respond to the previous speaker in saying that the Democrats must vote for term limits in order to pass it; I would just remind the gentleman from Illinois that he needs to get his leadership and his Republicans to vote for term limits, where the gentleman from Texas [Mr. DeLAY] is not going to vote for term limits; the gentleman from Illinois [Mr. HYDE] is not going to vote for term limits, the chairman of the Committee on the Judiciary; the gentleman from Louisiana [Mr. Livingston], chairman of the Committee on Appropriations, is not going to vote for term limits.

It is not the Democrats that are refusing to vote for term limits. It is the Republicans as a body that are not totally endorsing term limits and will be responsible for this matter not going through the House of Representatives.

Now, term limits, they think, is the answer to everything. Mexico has very strict term limits for their President, their Senate, and their House of Representatives. It certainly has not solved all the problems in Mexico, and people like Mr. Madison and Mr.Jefferson served this country valiantly and with courage and responsibility for up to 43 years.

We should not remove that responsibility from people in this country.

URGING SUPPORT FOR TERM LIMITS

(Mr. WHITE asked and was given permission to address the House for 1 minute.)

Mr. WHITE. Mr. Speaker, I have only been here for a short period of time, just 3 months, but in that short period of time I have learned something about term limits.

I have learned that there are lots of good people who have been in this House for a long period of time, people with experience who can add a lot to the debate, and if we pass term limits today, Mr. Speaker, some of those people will not be able to stay.

But, Mr. Speaker, for every single person we will lose because of term limits, there are thousands and thousands of other Americans who could serve equally well in this House, because no matter how much experience we have in the House, no matter how many Rhodes Scholars we have in the White House, the genius of our country resides in the people of this country, not in professional politicians.

That is why I have limited my own term. That is why I will vote for term limits.

Mr. Speaker, I ask my colleagues to show some humility. We need the wisdom of the American people in this House, and term limits is how we are going to get it.

A HISTORICAl DAY IN THE HOUSE OF REPRESENTATIVES

(Mr. CLEMENT asked and was given permission to address the House for 1 minute and to revise and extend his remarks.)

Mr. CLEMENT. Mr. Speaker, this is a historic day in the House. This will be the first vote in the House on term limits since the Framers of the Constitution rejected the idea over 200 years ago.

I believe term limits are not needed or necessary. Voters have the opportunity to limit our careers every 2 years. We have had a 52-percent turnover in the House of Representatives since 1990.

It is going to put much more power in the hands of the bureaucracy rather than the elected officials. And No. 5 [reason] is the large States really benefit at the expense of the smaller States such as Tennessee.

But with everything said and with my reservations about term limits, I will vote to let the people in Tennessee and the respective States decide whether term limits is in the best interests of the country. I will uphold the wishes of the people of my State and let them decide whether or not they wish to amend the Constitution even though I think it is a bad idea.

SUPPORT THE HILLEARY AMENDMENT

(Mrs. MYRICK asked and was given permission to address the House for 1 minute and to revise and extend her remarks.)

Mrs. MYRICK. Mr. Speaker, in my home State of North Carolina, stock car racing is a huge event.

In stock car racing the car driver has a pit crew. These are the guys who work on the engine, fill it up with gas, and keep the car running.

When a driver pulls into the pits to have his crew work on the car, the crew only has a few seconds to do their job.

They change the tires, fill it up, clean the windshield, and then they get out.

Mr. Speaker, the American public elected us to be their pit crew.

The 1994 elections attempted to put America back on the right track. Hard working Americans are driving this country, but they have chosen us to come up here, do a job and get out.

I am a proud sponsor of the House Joint Resolution 73, the Hilleary amendment which would impose a maximum 12-year limit on the terms of House and Senate Members.

However, this amendment would also respect term limits already established by 22 States nationwide, most of which are stricter.

Mr. Speaker, like many other freshman Republicans, I have also signed on to Mr. INGLIS' 6-year term limit amendment on House Members.

I have purposely signed on to more than one amendment to help ensure that term limits pass this House.

Mr.Speaker, let us put America back on the right track and pass term limits.

MAJORITY OF AMERICANS WANT TERM LIMITS

(Mr. HOKE asaked and was given permission to address the House for 1 minute.)

Mr. HOKE. Mr. Speaker, in my 1992 campaign, I said, "I am for term limits because I think it takes choices away from the voters." But the American people did choose. They chose by an overwhelming majority that they want term limits. It was their choice. Twenty-four and half million Americans have chosen term limits.

When you talk about choices for the voters, let us look at what happened in California. In California, the number of candidates running for office has increased by 40 percent since passage of term limits. That gives voters an awful lot more choices, does it not? Does it not increase the choices dramatically?

Mr. Speaker, the American people clearly want term limits. Republicans cannot do it alone. We need only half of the Democrats, we just need half of your caucus to vote for term limits. And the gentleman from Michigan's [Mr. DINGELL] own bill, we just need half of the Democrats to give the American people what they want, a more accountable citizen legislature and an end to legislative careerism.

OUR NATION IS BEST SERVED BY HAVING TERM LIMITS

(Mr. NORWOOD asked and was given permission to address the House for 1 minute.)

Mr. NORWOOD. Mr. Speaker, I would like to point out that I bow to the will of this body, my term-limits badge inside my coat, not on the outside.

Mr. Speaker, I ask my colleagues to consider the words of George Mason, a man whose vision was critical to our Bill of Rights. Mason said:

In order to restrain public officials from oppression, they should at fixed periods, be reduced to a private station and return into the body from which they were originally taken * * * where they might feel and participate in the burdens of the people.

Mr. Speaker, that means people here should be responsible for the payroll, their production should warrant what their income is, and people who have lived under the oppressive rules and regulations of the Federal Government. Mr. Speaker, Congress should be of the people, not its permanent representative. Mason knew that this Nation would be best served by having individuals who have lived as private citizens representing them in Congress. I urge my colleagues to vote for term limits.

Paulette G. Honeygosky

EIGHTY PERCENT OF AMERICANS SUPPORT TERM LIMITS
(Mr. KNOLLENBERG asked and was given permission to address the House for 1 minute and to revise and extend his remarks.)

Mr. KNOLLENBERG. Mr. Speaker, polls estimate, as everybody knows, that 80 percent of Americans support term limits. Yet I know there are some Republicans who do not, but there are some Democrats who, frankly, oppose, and have actively done so, for some time. Frustrated by 40 years of Democratic inaction and blatant obstruction to term limits, the American people were forced to take this battle to the ballot box, State by State, in a grassroots effort to circumvent an arrogant Congress that thought it knew better than those people it represented.

The makeup of today's Congress is very different, in large part because of the term-limit movement. The new majority believes the people have a right to be heard, and that is why this GOP-led Congress is bringing a historic first ever vote on term limits to the floor of the House today.

For those Democrats sitting on the fence on term limits, just talking about those on the fence, look back at last year's elections. Many of your colleagues who fought against the will of the people, about thirty-five of them, are not here. They are now watching this debate as observers instead of Members of Congress.

The way I see it, we either get your vote on term limits today or we will get your seat in 1996. Think about it.

MEMBERS OF CONGRESS SHOULD RETURN HOME AND MIX WITH THE PEOPLE

(Mr. BRYANT of Tennessee asked and was given permission to address the House for 1 minute and to revise and extend his remarks.)

Mr. Speaker, I rise to speak in favor of term limits as a freshman Congressman who has been here 2 months and who has pledged to my district that I will limit my stay to 12 years.

I have taken voluntary term limits.

Mr. Speaker, the case for term limits is a simple one. As one of the Founding Fathers, Roger Sherman of Connecticut, put it, members of the legislature, "ought to return home and mix with the people." He warned that if they did not, "they would acquire the habits of the place, which might differ from those of their constituents."

How right he was. Once in office a survival instinct takes hold and nothing becomes as important as winning the next election. Members forget why they were sent to Washington.

Mr. Speaker, term limits have been bottled up for years by the Democratic leadership, but it will finally come to the House floor today. But it will not pass unless we convince about half of the Democrats to vote with the over 80 percent of the Republicans to support term limits.

I would hate to see term limits fail because of a lack of support from my colleagues on the Democratic side. We need only 50 percent of them to vote with us on this. Let us not let term limits fall victim to a lack of bipartisan effort. Let us seize the moment. Let us pass term limits.

TERM LIMITS CONSTITUTIONAL AMENDMENT

The SPEAKER pro tempore. Pursuant to House Resolution 116 and rule XXIII, the Chair declares the House in the Committee of the Whole House on the State of the Union for the consideration of the House Joint Resolution, House Joint Resolution 73.

IN THE COMMITTEE OF THE WHOLE

Accordingly, the House resolved itself into the Committee of the Whole House on the State of the Union for the consideration of joint resolution (H.J.Res. 73) proposing an amendment to the Constitution of the United States with respect to the number of terms of office of Members of the Senate and the House of Representatives, with Mr. KLUG in the chair.

The Clerk read the title of the joint resolution.

The CHAIRMAN. Pursuant to the rule, the joint resolution is considered as having been read the first time.

The CHAIRMAN. Under this rule, the gentleman from Florida [Mr. CANADY] will be reognized for one and a half hours, and the gentleman from Michigan [Mr. CONYERS] will be recognized for one and a half hours.

The Chair recognizes the gentleman from Florida [Mr. CANADY].

Mr. CANADY of Florida. Mr. Chairman, I yield myself such time as I may consume.

Mr. Chairman, this is a historic day. Since the convening of the first Congress on March 4, 1789, more than 180 term-limit proposals have been introduced. Until today, however, there has never been a debate or vote on a term limits measure in the U.S. House of Representatives. Today's debate is long overdue.

We are taking up this important issue today because an overwhelming majority of the public supports - and is demanding - term limits for members of Congress. This past November, the voters of 7 States adopted or strengthened limits on terms for Members of the U.S. House and Senate, bringing the number of States with congressional term liimits to 22. Twenty-one of those States have imposed term limits through ballot initiatives - with the people speaking directly and unequivocally in favor of term limits.

It is clear that voters want more than the party in power to change. The people want the power structure in Washington to change. The American people know that there is too much power here in Washington intruding upon their lives and restricting their ability to make intelligent common sense decisions about how best to solve their own problems.

The executive branch is huge and imposing. The judiciary is intrusive, and the Congress continues to create a larger body of law for the executive branch to enforce and the judiciary to interpret.

It is an unfortunate consequence of long-term service in Congress that Members, even those with the best of intentions, too often begin to think that the power of the Federal Government can be used to solve every problem. The longer a Member stays in Washington, the more likely the Member will view Washington as the fount of all wisdom.

There are enough people in Washington who think the Government can solve everyone's problems. This Nation needs representatives who have a fresh outlook and the necessary real-world experience to solve problems - many of which ironically, have been created by the overreaching of the Federal Government.

Congress has become too much like a permanent class of professional legislators who can use the powers of the Federal Government to perpetuate their own careers. There are many incentives which combine to turn Members of Congress into career legislators. Term limits will break the power of entrenched incumbency. It will give us representatives who put serving the interests of the people and advancing the good of the Nation ahead of perpetrating their own legislative careers.

The American people want a more competitive electoral system. That is one important reason the public so strongly supports term limits.

While the 1994 elections changed the party in control of the Congress, the overwhelming power and the benefits of incumbency remained. Ninety percent of House incumbents who sought reelection were successful. Of those incumbents who lost, half had not gained the full advantages of incumbency because they had only served one term. In the Senate, 92 percent of the incumbents who ran for reelection were successful.

The American people also want to rein in the Federal Government. That's another major reason the people keep pushing for term limits on Members of Congress.

Term limits would reduce the power of the Federal Government by eliminating the permanent class of career legislators - reducing the power of incumbency and seniority and making legislators more responsive to the interests of the American people. Term limits would restore a sense of proportion to politicians, and therefore to the Federal Government.

Some argue that term limits will undermine effective and responsible Government - that term limits in effect will turn the Congress over to a gang of amateurs.

I believe that these critics misunderstand the true meaning of representation in a democracy such as ours. Their arguments are eloquently refuted by Daniel Boorstein, the historian and former Librarian of Congress, in an essay entitled, "The Amateur Spirit and Its Enemies." Mr. Boorstein writes:

The true leader is an amateur in the proper, original sense of the word. The amateur, from the Latin word for "love", does something for the love of it. He pursues his enterprise not for money, not to please the crowd, not for professional prestige or for assured promotion and retirement at the end - but because he loves it. Aristocracies are governed by people born to govern totalitarian societies by people who make ruling their profession, but our representative government must be led by people never born to govern, temporaily drawn from the community and sooner or later sent back home.

Mr.Boorstein goes on to conclude:

The more complex and gigantic our government, the more essential that the layman's point of view have eloquent voices. The amateur spirit is a distinctive virtue of democracy. Every year, as professions and bureaucracies increase in power, it becomes more difficult - yet more urgent - to keep that spirit alive.

By enacting term limits we will be doing our part to keep alive this distinctive virtue of democracy. We will make certain that representatives understand the needs and wants of the people, because they will have been a part of their world - living and working among them - without the privileges and trappings which elevate and isolate career politicians.

Members will come to Washington knowing that they will not be able to establish permanent careers here. Members will come to Washington to serve their districts and the Nation - not to become part of the Washington establishment.

That is what the people of this country want. That's the kind of system they yearn for. And that is the kind of system they deserve.

As Members of this House it is our responsibility to listen to the American people. This is their Government. They pay the taxes. They fight the wars. How can we in good conscience turn a deaf ear to their demand for term limits?

How can we ignore the unequivocal message that comes to us from all across this great land?

How can we stand in the way of the change that overwhelming majorities have supported in State after State?

The issue before this House today is this: Will we or will we not listen to the people of the United States?

I urge my colleagues to listen to the people and to support the constitutional amendment limiting congressional terms.

Mr. Chairman, I reserve the balance of my time.

Mr. CONYERS. Mr. Chairman, for purposes of debate only, I yield 30 minutes to the gentleman from Connecticut [Mr. SHAYS], and I ask unanimous consent that he be able to control that time.

The CHAIRMAN. Is there any objection to the request of the gentleman from Michigan?

There was no objection.

Mr. CONYERS. Mr. Chairman, I yield myself such time as I may consume.
(Mr. CONYERS asked and was given permission to revise and extend his remarks.)

Mr. CONYERS. Mr. Chairman and my colleagues, we have now reached that point in time in the plank of the Republicans' *Contract With America* which seeks to turn the Congress against itself. Like many of the other provisions of the much ballyhood contract, Mr. Chairman, the proposed term limits amendment has really very little to do with substance. Like the balanced budget amendment and the line-item veto, this debate concerns mere procedure more than anything else. It does nothing to create more jobs, nothing to increase our citizens' standard of living, and nothing to reduce our trade deficit.

Collectively these Republican procedural proposals say to the American people in effect that we, the Congress, can no longer be trusted to govern this country, that we must give the courts the power to balance the budget, and the President the power to cut spending, and today the Republicans would have us say that we cannot even trust the Members of this body to handle what little legislative responsibilties may remain with us as the second branch of Government. The irony is that these transfers in power from the legislative branch are being proposed at the very time the Republicans have achieved majority status.

Well, I must respectfully disagree with those who say Congress is incapable of legislating, and while this may be a radical idea, I continue to have faith in the scheme of Government that was laid out in our Constitution more than 2 centuries ago. The founding Fathers considered this question and they unanimously rejected term limits at that time. I fully agree with James Madison who wrote that term limits "would be a diminution of the inducements to good behavior *** [and the Nation would be deprived] of the experience and wisdom gained by an incumbent."

Mr. Chairman, I ask, where else is experience trashed as it will be during this debate: Where else will people who have gained from working on the job, who are being reelected and confirmed in their office on 2-year period intervals, would such a notion as this be considered worthy of all the attention and furor that it will shortly receive?

I also continue to have faith in the fundamental good judgment of the American voters who have already the power to impose term limits. We face the voters every 2 years; does anyone in this Chamber need to be reminded of that? The Senators, every 6 years. I do not think it a good idea to deny these voters the right to elect the person that they think best represents their interests, even though he or she may have received their support in years prior. This would turn the very basic principle of democracy on its head.

I think the voters of Texas knew what they were doing when they reelected Sam Rayburn year after year after year, and the people of North Carolina knew what they were doing when they repeatedly returned Sam Ervin to office. His wise counsel and well-reasoned judgments helped steer this country through a dangerous Constitutional crisis that I recall very vividly. And what Member would have wanted to deny the voters of Florida the opportunity to reelect Claude Pepper so that he could fight for Social Security and health care benefits?

May I also remind those who support term limits that the notion of a career Congress which they decry so vehemently is more myth than anything else. Membership in the House and the Senate is remade every decade. In the early 1980's, a full three-fourths of Senators and Representatives had served less than 12 years, and more than one-half of the current Members of the House at this moment were elected on or after 1990.

So, the best safeguard we have against rampant special interest abuse are the Members who have been around long enough to know the ropes and know where the bodies are buried. If the voters understood that the effect of term limits would be a massive transfer of power to the permanent bureaucracy of congressional and executive branch staff as well as to corporate and foreign lobbyists, they might not be quite so enamored of the idea. Given a choice between an elected official beholden to the voters and an unelected bureaucrat, I think the voters would prefer to place their trust in the elected official every time.

Term limits are the worst possible example of cheap bumper sticker politics run amok. We have spent enough time kicking ourselves in the face and looking to other branches of government to solve our problems, and I say to my colleagues on both sides of the aisle, let's stop wasting time with these procedural distractions and return to the business of running the country and improving the lives of citizens that we claim to represent.

Mr. Chairman, I reserve the balance of my time.

Mr. CANADY of Florida. Mr. Chairman, I yield 4 minutes to the gentleman from Tennessee [Mr. DUNCAN].

Mr. DUNCAN. Mr. Chairman, I rise to speak against term limits, and I thank the gentleman from Florida for yielding me this time.

I realize that term limits are very popular, and that they will receive a very large vote in favor here today.

I realize that in some ways I am tilting at windmills here. But I also know that very few people realize how much turnover is already occurring in this body.

The people have elected 203 new Members in just the last 2 years. Let me repeat that: 203 Members - almost half the House - have begun their service just since January 1993.

There were 110 freshmen elected 2 years ago - and 6 more in special elections in between - and 87 more freshmen in the last election.

If ever there was a proposal that corrected a problem that does not exist, term limits must be that proposal.

Of all the truly serious problems this country faces, turnover in the Congress is not one of them.

Not only are we having record turnover in the Congress, that same thing is happening in the elective offices all across the Nation. So I emphasize once more - term limits correct a problem that does not exist.

Second, term limits simply fly in the face of common sense. In no other area do we regard experience as a bad thing.

Does it make sense to go to a great teacher, or nurse, or architect, or whatever, and say, "We know you are doing a great job, but you have been here 6 years or 8 years, so your time is up."

Electing good new people to office makes sense. Re-electing people who are doing good jobs makes sense. Establishing arbitrary term limits - which everyone admits will force many outstanding people out of office - just does not make sense.

Third, we would have lost some of the greatest service ever performed for this Nation if we had already had term limits.

Senator Howard Baker from my State could not have served as the leader of the Senate - probably some of his greatest service to the country.

NEWT GINGRICH could not now be Speaker, because he is in his 17th year of service.

Roll Call, the newspaper that covers the Congress, pointed out Monday that Great Britain would have been deprived of the service of Winston Churchill during World War II.

Fourth, term limits were specifically considered and rejected by our Founding Fathers.

I am one of the most conservative Members of this House. I know that most conservatives support term limits.

But there is nothing conservative about term limits. These are very radical proposals. They would change over 200 years of constitutional history and precedent.

More importantly, they are very undemocratic - with a small "d". They really take away another right of our people - the right to vote for whomever they please.

Fifth, and finally, term limits will strengthen the power of the unelected - the bureaucrats, the lobbyists, the committee staff.

We already have a Government that is of, by, and for the bureaucrats, instead of one that is of, by, and for the people. Term limits will make this situation worse.

Term limits have risen as an outcry against a big, wasteful,intrusive, bureaucratic Government.

The people have the intelligence and good sense to know who is voting for big Government and who is not.

The best way to bring about effective change is the old-fashioned way — through our electoral process that has served this country so well for so many years.

The worst possible thing to do now, during a time of great change anyway, is to try out some radical, arbitrary gimmick like term limits, which corrects a problem that does not exist.

Mr. CONYERS. Mr. Chairman, I yield 5 minutes to the distinguished gentleman from Illinois [Mr. Gutierrez],who, although he is not a member of the committee, has done an outstanding job in working on this subject.

Mr. GUTIERREZ. Mr. Chairman, I rise this morning aware of the fact that there are many different audiences listening.

There is the audience in this House - Members who have various opinions about this issue, who feel strongly about the debate we are having, who have studied the pros and cons.

There are some - like my friends on this side of the aisle like Mr. CONYERS - who have gone about it the right way.

They have taken a close look at the legal opinions.

71

They have taken a close look at the Constitution that we live by.

And more importantly, they have taken a close look within themselves and their own conscience to decide whether they support term limits.

Like them I have decided that I cannot support term limits as they have been written by the Republicans.

Unfortunately, there are others in this Chamber - mostly on the other side of the aisle - who have decided to look at public opinion polls rather than look at the Constitution.

They have watched focus groups rather than focus on the real impact of this resolution.

They have decided to listen more closely to the angry voices of talk radio rather than the subtle, eloquent and ancient voices of our founding Fathers who thought that the people had the right to decide whom to elect to Congress.

In fact, the Founding Fathers did - in their wisdom - write term limits into the Constitution. Term limits that work. Every 2 years, your term is up. You want an extension, you go to the people - the people - and ask for their approval.

Now, it is obvious that the Republicans understand that reality. They realize that they need to be reelected. Otherwise, we would not have the ranting and raving and pandering and posturing that you are going to hear from them today.

So I very much want to speak to my colleagues here today, and engage with them in a meaningful debate.

Meanwhile, thanks to the magic of cable television, there is an audience all around the country with whom I can speak this morning. There are people in my district in Illinois listening and watching.

And for them I am taking a stand against fake phony term limits.

But, there are also people in districts far away whom I would also like to address.

I would like people in districts like Florida's Eighth District to listen closely. Not just to my words, but to those of your own Representative.

Now, I hope you do not think I am picking on your Congressman, Mr. McCOLLUM. I trust that you sent him here with some good reason.

But, Mr. McCOLLUM has thrust himself into this term limits debate. He has done so with some intensity.

And all I can say is, when you do that - when you start slinging arrows, do not be surprised when one comes back at you.

So, here it comes.

He, McCOLLUM, is a chief sponsor of a bill to limit Members to a term of 12 years.

He, McCOLLUM, was elected in 1980.

It is now 1995.

Now, you do the math, and you figure out that if Mr. McCOLLUM really believed what he said, there would be a very simple way for him to enact the 12-year term limits. Walk away.

Now, you might be inclined to think that Mr. McCOLLUM will at least support the amendment that I will speak on later today to make term limits retroactive.

Nope. Not him.

Even so, let us just listen to the words of Mr. McCOLLUM, who today is proud to tell us that he sponsors a resolution for a 12-year term limit.

He said: "Those of us who believe in term limits * * * need to stay longer, unfortunately, because the system is the way it is."

If you have been here that long, you are the system. You are the system that you say needs changing.

Now, let us go on, because there is also an audience in the Sixth District of Georgia listening to me.

Today I want to send a special message to them:

I want to inform you that your Congressman, Mr. GINGRICH - whom you first elected in 1978 - supports limiting members to 12 years of service.

In a press conference endorsing the 12-year limit, the Speaker, now in his 17th year, said, "The balance of power in favor of professional politicians as incumbents * * * has made a mockery of the process of open elections."

So,that must mean that each election held in Georgia's Sixth District since 1990 - when Mr. GINGRICH's 12 years were up - has been a mockery.

If I lived in Georgia, I would be concerned to hear that I had voted in a mockery of an election.

In fact - three of them, since 1990.

Now, I have heard a lot of the people talk about the Speaker and his problems with GOPAC.

Well, today, I am not going to talk about GOPAC.

But I am going to say go back, as in go back to Georgia, because the 12-year limit that you want to impose on everyone else has long ago passed for you.

Go back, as in how do you go back to your district every week - and I know that he does, because I see him on t.v. teaching that course on "Saving the Western World" or whatever it is called - but, how do you go back to your district every week and tell folks that you support a 12-year limit, but you are going on serving well beyond that.

No, I am not going to say GOPAC but I am going to say go back - as in how do you go back on your word, Mr. Speaker?

Mr. GINGRICH said that without these changes, the congressional campaigns are a "mockery".

Well, thanks to his Republicans and their empty term limits rhetoric, they are making mockery of Congress.

What is a mockery?

The dictionary says "an action of ridicule * * * false * * * and imitation."

That is what today's debate is.

Ah, but there is an answer.

A way to ensure that the political power in this country is given back to the people who deserve to have it. The men and women who work hard and play by the rules. And that is with serious, substantive campaign finance reform.

Campaign finance reform insures that an incumbent must earn - and continue to earn - his or her seat in the body, rather than act like they own it.

Nobody owns a seat in this House.

But, as long as we debate phony issues like term limits, and avoid real issues like campaign finance reform, we make it possible for lobbyists and big-dollar contributors to own Members.

In their contract, this was part of the Republicans' so-called Citizen Legislature Act.

You want a legislature that belongs to the citizens? Good. Let us put limits on the time we spend raising money and hustling for votes.

Campaign finance reform is the answer.

Term limits is not.

ANNOUNCEMENT BY THE CHAIRMAN

THE CHAIRMAN. The Chair wishes to remind our visitors in the gallery that no expressions on their part are allowed.

Mr. SHAYS. Mr. Chairman, to begin debate, I yield 4 minutes to the distinguished gentleman from New York [Mr. KING], one Member who is strongly opposed to term limits.

Mr. KING. Mr. Chairman, I thank the gentleman for yielding me this time.

Mr. Chairman, I rise in total opposition to term limits. I oppose term limits because they are undemocratic and because they represent the ultimate in elitism.

For someone from some other part of the country to come to my district and tell my voters they cannot vote for me just because I happen to have been in office for 6 years or 8 years or 12 years is the ultimate insider mentality. They are saying that they know more than the average voter in the average district around this country.

Perhaps in their districts people want to elect part-time farmers or barnyard philosophers. That is fine. Let them elect those people. Let them send them here to Congress. But my point is that it is up to each voter in each district to decide what person they want to elect to Congress.

I must say that while it is very seldom that I agree with my friend, the gentleman from Illinois [Mr.GUTIERREZ], there is a lot to be said for the logic of retroactivity. My feeling is that we should only amend the Constitution if it represents an ultimate truth, something about which there can be no debate. For instance, the 13th amendment abolished slavery. Now, would those who favor term limits have followed the logic in the 1860's of saying, "I am opposed to slavery, but I'm not going to free my slaves until the amendment is adopted" or "I'm going to continue being a slave holder because the 13th amendment isn't adopted yet"?

Of course not. If it is wrong, if it is immoral, if it somehow tears away at our country not to have term limits, then lead by example - go home, because otherwise what you are saying is that this is just a political issue that we use to get elected. And as a Republican, I am very, very concerned about this entire pernicious pattern of pandering and posturing by Members who seem to have an unquenchable quest or an unquenchable thirst for self-flagellation. It is part of an overall pattern where they are denouncing everything about the Congress, denouncing being a politician, denouncing being a person committed to making change in government.

My feeling or my strong belief is that those of us who say we want change, what we are really doing, those of us who support term limits are saying that the voters in the districts are not smart enough to elect the proper Members to Congress, and what could be more elitist, what could be more anti-democratic, what could be more of an inside-the-beltway mentality than to be denying the voters of individual districts the right to elect the Members of their choice?

Just think, I say to the Republicans, my fellow Republicans, of some of the outstanding Members who would not have been elected if we had had term limits. The voters of Ohio would not have been allowed to reelect Robert Taft to his third term in the U.S. Senate. The voters of Illinois would not have been able to elect Everett Dirksen. The voters of Kansas would not have been allowed to reelect ROBERT DOLE. And on the Democratic side, outstanding leaders such as Sam Rayburn would not have been allowed to return to Congress because someone in Washington said that it is wrong for the people in Texas or Ohio or Illinois to select the person they want to represent them in Congress.

I am probably the last person in this body who could be accused of being an Anglophile. However, the point is made about Winston Churchill. He was a man who served over 40 years in the British Parliament. Are we saying it was wrong or that it was immoral for Winston Churchill to be in the Parliament at the time of World War II?

Who among us would be better qualified? Would it have been that part-time farmer from some State? Would he have been a better Speaker? Maybe he would have, but let the voters in that district decide.

Also one of the main arguments that we have used against Congress in our incessant campaigns against Congress has been the fact that staffs are too powerful. Nothing could make staffs more powerful than to have Members rotating in and out and having a permanent unelected body of staff deciding the legislation, deciding the procedures, deciding the process.

I strongly believe that for a Congress to be effective we need a whole range of Members in this Congress. We need the institutional memory of someone like a HENRY HYDE or a JOE MOAKLEY.

The CHAIRMAN. The time of the gentleman from New York [Mr. KING] has expired.

Mr. FRANK of Massachusetts. Mr. Chairman, I yield 30 additional seconds to the gentleman from New York [Mr. KING].

Mr. KING. Mr. Chairman, I will take the 30 seconds from Mr. SHAYS.

Mr. FRANK of Massachusetts. Mr. Chairman, I would point out to the gentleman that Mr. SHAYS got the 30 seconds from us, so if he wants to go through the middleman, he is entitled.

Mr. KING. I have enough trouble with my own party. It is easier if I get it from Mr. SHAYS.

Mr. Chairman, I thank the gentleman from Massachusetts [Mr. FRANK] very much for his munificence.

In conclusion, Mr. Chairman, to be a real representative body what we need is a wide range of elected officials, but we should not be imposing our will on who those elected officials are. It should be the genius of the American people to decide that we need a person of experience like a HENRY HYDE and we need a person like my good friend, the gentleman from South Carolina, Mr. BOB INGLIS who is going to be gone in 3 years. But that is up to the people to decide, not for us to say who should be changed or who should not be changed. Let the American people decide that. They decided that in 1994 when they overwhelmingly rejected Democrats and elected Republicans. We are our own best argument against term limits.

Mr. CANADY of Florida. Mr. Chairman, I yield 5 minutes to the gentleman from South Carolina [Mr. INGLIS].

Mr. INGLIS of South Carolina. Mr. Chairman, I thank the gentleman for yielding me the time, and I rise today to mark this historic occasion of finally having the opportunity to discuss, debate, and vote on term limits on the floor of the House of Representatives.

What a wonderful day it is. After a long time working for this, we finally get the opportunity. It is a great thing. What a difference an election can make.

In the last Congress we had a Speaker who sued us in the State of Washington to prevent us from enacting term limits. This time we have a Speaker who is working with us to bring this to a vote.

I rise today, Mr. Chairman, to point out the basic case for term limits and then to answer several of the objections.

First, the basic case: The average American, as the Members can see here by my chart, keeps his or her job 6 years. The average Member of Congress keeps his or her job 8 years. That is not terribly long, and a lot of speakers will point out that some 200 Members are relatively new.

But here is the critical statistic: The average Members of the leadership who we all know run this place have kept their jobs for an average of 22 years. This tells the story of why we need term limits.

Let me point out another chart that tells the story of why we need term limits. Of course, we had all this discussion, and we will hear plenty of it today from the opponents of term limits, about the fact that we have had such a massive turnover in this body. But let us ask where the turnover came from. The turnover came from open seat elections. Relatively few Members have lost their attempts to be elected, and let me show that to the Members by this chart.

In 1990, 96 percent of those who wanted to come back came back. In 1992, it went down a little bit. 88 percent of those who wanted to come back came back. In 1994, the election that got us this management change, and I am very thankful, as I just stated, for that management change, because now we have an opportunity to debate term limits, 90 percent of those of us who wanted to come back were reelected. That I think tells the story of a permanent Congress, a Congress that becomes out of touch with the people back home.

Now, about the issue of what the States have done, as you can see here, some 22 States have decided to limit terms. That I think is an indication of the strength of support out there and why it is that this is finally long overdue and now thankfully is on the floor of the House of Representatives.

In the time that remains, let me address a couple of the major objections to term limits. First, the bureaucracy will run the place. Let me ask the other Members of Congress today to address this question. If you are talking civil servants, there is no way a Member of Congress can deal with a civil servant. How about your personal staff and how many do you have on your staff? I have got 15, and 2 part-time folks. The people at home direct a whole lot of people. In small businesses they may have 100 people they direct. In big corporations they may have thousands of people they direct. So we cannot make too much of our job here. Let us not think too highly of ourselves. It is a relatively small operation. There are only 15 or so in our offices, 18 if you have the full complement and spending all the taxpayers' money and 4 part-time people. It is a small operation. Let us be honest.

So the bureaucracy, you cannot control the civil servants now, except by controlling their appropriations. You can control your own office, because there are so few people in there.

Now, second objection: We are going to lose talent. How are we going to lose the talent? If a talented Member of this House wants to run for Governor, nobody in the term limit effort begrudges them that. We would encourage them to run for Governor. If a talented Member of the Senate wants to run for President, we encourage them to run for President. We are not going to lose the talent; we are going to redirect it. All the folks we are hearing about we are going to lose, they might be the President of the United States if we forced them out of here, or might be a great Senator, or maybe a Governor. We will force them over there.

The third objection that my good friend just mentioned speaking before me is do not tell my people who they can vote for. Do not limit their choices. Well, who are you speaking for? Eighty percent of the American people want term limits. They told you that. They tell you every town meeting. They tell you in every poll taken in your district. Who are you speaking for? The 20 percent?

They are giving you a message. They want to limit you. They are just being fairly polite about it by not telling you to your face, but they are telling you in every opinion poll 80 percent of us want term limits.

So when you stand here and say do not tell my people how they cannot reelect me, they are trying to tell you they do not want to reelect you after a period of time.

Mr. FRANK of Massachusetts. Mr. Chairman, I yield 2 and a half minutes to the gentleman from Maryland [Mr. WYNN].

Mr. WYNN. Mr. Chairman, I thank the gentleman for yielding.

Mr. Chairman, I would like to talk about term limits, and maybe debunk some of the myths that have been put out about why term limits are such a good idea.

Now, the first argument that you hear is that well, the majority of people like it. You just heard 80 percent of the people like term limits. Well, they have an easy solution. Do not vote for us. The fact of the matter is, the people right now have that option. All those people who do not like the incumbent can not vote for the incumbent. But if you think about it, ladies and gentlemen, the point of the matter is this is not a popularity contest. A lot of the majority at one point in time thought slavery was a good idea. You could probably get a majority today to abolish all taxes. That does not dispose of the issue. Clearly we need more thought on this issue.

Second, you hear what we need is a citizen legislature. We are all citizens. It does not matter whether you have been here 2, 10, or 20 years, we are all citizens. But my point is, being in the legislature is not a hobby. It is not a lark. It is a job with a tremendous amount of responsibility. I am going into my third year, and I have to tell you, it is an awesome responsibility, and there is a very high learning curve. You do not manage a multitrillion-dollar budget by walking in off the street.

People want to say, particularly on the Republican side of the aisle, well, you ought to run Government like a business. Ladies and gentlemen, you know, every business cherishes its talented people. There is no corporation in America that says after you have been here 6 years and begun to learn the business or after you have been managing for 12 years and things are going well, we are going to kick you out the door. It does not work that way. Yes, run Government like a business, keep talented people there. At least give them the opportunity to be retained.

Third, you hear about incumbency. First of all, there are 83 new Members in this body, so incumbents are not winning all the races. The gentleman says most of the incumbents still won anyway. Yes, people like me, who are incumbents the last time around, who were freshmen incumbents. There are over 100 in my class. Most of us did win. That is not an indictment of this system to suggest that incumbents win. That is the reasonable outcome.

Finally, there is the issue of career politicians. Let me state emphatically, there is nothing wrong with a career in politics, if you do a good job, if your people think you do a good job, and if they elect you.

Mr. Chairman, I think the people ought to have the right to select the person that they want. That is the only issue in this debate, the right of American people to decide in their individual district and their individual community if they want to retain someone or if they want to oust them. I trust the wisdom of the American people to make that decision on election day, and that is why I believe we do not need term limits."

Mr. CANADY of Florida. Mr. Chairman, I yield 4 and a half minutes, to the gentleman from Wisconsin [Mr. SENSEN-BRENNER].

Mr. SENSENBRENNER. Mr. Chairman, I rise in opposition to this joint resolution, and I urge the membership to defeat each of the substitutes that will come before us later on today. Term limits, in my opinion, are a bad idea. They are anti-democratic, and I think that they will upset the balance of power and checks and balances that the Framers of our Constitution so delicately devised and which have served the United States of America so well for over 200 years.

The Constitution of the United States should not tell the voters who they cannot vote for. That is a Government law that limits the choice of the voters and tells the voters that if someone has served for 6 or 8 or 12 years, they are no longer qualified to serve in the Congress of the United States, no matter how distinguished their service has been, no matter how much they represented the viewpoints of the majority of their constituents, and no matter how honest and forthright they are. I think that is wrong.

Second, term limits will end up strengthening the hand of the executive and judicial branches at the expense of Congress. Many of the more ardent supporters of term limits say that they support limiting terms because they wish to weaken the legislative branch of Government, the Congress of the United States. But if one stops and thinks about that argument, it weakens the only branch that is completely elected by the people of this country. Every Senator and Representative is an elected official. But in the Executive and Judicial Branches, only the President is elected, and those are the two branches of Government that will become stronger proportionately as Congress is weakened by term limits.

In fact, term limits will actually make Representative and Senators more distant from their constituents, because they will no longer have the incentive to go back home and face their people and find out what their people are thinking in order to win reelection.

The third problem with term limits is that it will effectively place control of the House of Representatives in the hands of the four largest State delegations. That means that those who represent the other 46 States, no matter how talented they are, are not going to be able to achieve the respect, to get on good committees, and to achieve the knowledge that goes with being on the strong and powerful committees, and will be relegated to serving on the committees that are of much lower priority.

I just look at my own State, where Les Aspin and DAVID OBEY, Henry Reuss and Clement Zablocki on the Democratic side, and Melvin Laird and John Byrnes and William Steiger on the Republican side have served with distinction. But they were never able to hit their prime until they had been here for 10 or 12 years, because they had not gotten the respect and the chits from their other colleagues in order to get into positions of influence.

Finally, term limits and changing the Constitution will not change human nature. Human beings are those who are elected by the people to represent them in the Congress of the United States. The reward for doing a good job in this business is reelection, and that is an incentive that drives us to represent our people and to go back home and listen to what the people are saying.

I am afraid that with term limits we would become much like Mexico, which is a government that has a term limit of one term on all of their elected officials. If you do not have to go back home, then you start looking for the next job right away. Every contact with the lobbyists then becomes a contact with a potential future employer. As it stands now, no Senator or Representative starts looking for the next job until they decide to retire or the voters decide that question for them.

With term limits, you are going to have people looking forward to the next job right from the very beginning. That is going to end up corrupting the system of government that we have to an even greater extent than it is now.

Please vote against term limits, uphold the Constitution of the United States, and uphold the checks and balances which have served our country so well.

Mr. FRANK of Massachusetts. Mr. Chairman, at her request, I yield 30 seconds to the gentlewoman from Oregon [Ms. FURSE].

Ms. FURSE. Mr. Chairman, I am rising in support of the term limit bill. I introduced a term limits bill identical to the one that Oregon passed. I want to say to my Republican colleague, the gentleman from New York [Mr. KING], he said Washington should not dictate. No, Washington should not. And it is not Washington who is dictating, it is the voters. The voters of Oregon overwhelmingly voted in favor of term limits, and I support the term limits bill.

Mr. SHAYS. Mr. Chairman, I yield 3 minutes to the gentleman from Illinois [Mr. PORTER].

Mr. PORTER. Mr. Chairman, it is amazing to me that anyone can believe that if only we can correct the faulty Constitution our Founders gave us by adding term limits, all our problems will be solved.

In 1787, the American Constitution was a revolutionary document, placing, for the first time in human history, its faith in the individual judgment of ordinary people as our governing force. Now some would abandon faith in the judgment of the people and urge an artificial restraint.

The Founders debated the issue of term limits at the constitutional convention and ultimately decided that the sole responsibility for choosing the people who would represent them should be left to the people, and not be controlled or limited by the Government. Thomas Jefferson said it best in a letter to William Charles Jarvis on September 28, 1820:

I know no safe depository of the ultimate power of the society but the people themselves; and if we think them not enlightened enough to exercise their control with a wholesome discretion, the remedy is not to take it from them, but to inform their discretion.

Our problems do not lie with a poorly written Constitution. They lie with our failure to live up to the trust placed in us by the founders. The solution is not to remove the trust, but for the people to fully inform themselves and fully participate in the electoral process as the founders envisioned. That has happened with a vengeance in the last two elections. Today, over half the House of Representatives has served less than 4 years. Congress is today a dynamic body, responsive to the people - without changing the Constitution.

Those who today urge support for term limits have it wrong. The founders, who debated term limits extensively in 1787, got it right the first time. Leave it to the people.

Mr. CANADY of Florida. Mr. Chairman, I yield 6 minutes to the gentleman from Florida [Mr. McCOLLUM].

MR. McCOLLUM. Mr. Chairman, I thank the gentleman for yielding.

Mr. Chairman, this is truly a historic day, the first time in the history of the U.S. House of Representatives that we are here to have a debate and vote on limiting the terms of Members of the U.S. House and Senate. It is something a lot of us have wanted to do for a long time, but we have never had that opportunity under the previous administration and the 40 years of Democrat control. But we have it here today. Now we need to take advantage of it.

We need to answer in this term limit debate two questions: Are congressional term limits a good idea; and, if so, what version is best to place in the U.S. Constitution?

The answer to the first question is clearly yes. The fact that nearly 80 percent of the American people favor term limits may alone be reason enough to enact them. But this begs the question. While there are numerous reasons for the support, the most profound go to the need to change the institution of Congress itself and the attitude of those who serve. When the Founding Fathers wrote the Constitution, they could not have foreseen the full-time year-round Congress of today. They never envisioned a Federal Government as large and complex as it is now. They viewed Congressmen as citizen legislators who spent only a couple of months every year legislating and the rest of the time at home conducting their personal business.

Indeed for over 100 years, most House Members served two terms or less and only in this half century has Congress become a year-round, full-time job.

The chart that I have here explains this pretty clearly. We have had a number of speakers this morning talking about the fact that we have had turnover recently in the last two elections. The problem is historically, if you look at the chart, you can see in the first 100 years of the Nation, we had very few Members who served nearly as long. Now they are serving a lot longer and those in the blue line on this chart who run for reelection are being reelected overwhelmingly, very high percentages today on the far end of that chart. So statistical norms show that we are in a period of time far different from what the Founding Fathers could have envisioned.

   With these fundamental institutional changes has come a change in the attitude of Members serving in Congress. Most Members have no outside earned income, and many are prohibited by law from practicing their professions. As a consequence, it is only natural that a great many Members view Congress as a career and are motivated to protect themselves from reelection challenges by far more than the simple desire to continue to serve their country. They see these facts: a seniority system which generally rewards length of service and the power of incumbents seeking reelection.

   Consequently many vote with the primary concern being how the vote will affect their reelection chances rather than what is best for the country.

   This concern with reelection frequently translates into votes to please every interest group. Virtually every budget item has a constituency in each congressional district. The Congressman knows that if he or she votes against the wishes of that constituency he risks their votes in the next election and the best way to get reelected is to avoid displeasing any interest group no matter its size. Votes, not campaign contributions, are the real issue. Hence, no amount of campaign finance reform will solve this problem.

   Enactment of term limits is the only way to alter this attitude. With term limits in place, those coming into Congress will know that they have only a limited period of time in the House or Senate.

   Most will not come with a career attitude. While still concerned with reelection, inevitably there will be less conscious or subconscious pressure to vote to please every interest group. This cannot help but make balanced budgets more likely and lead to decisions more favorable to the citizenry as a whole than to a collection of interest groups.

   Term limits will also mean a permanent end to chairmen who can control a committee for 15 or 20 years. It will guarantee fresh new faces and ideas regularly coming to Washington.

   Of course, there will be some loss of experience and institutional wisdom. It is a necessary tradeoff. With thousands of talented Americans available to fill the shoes of those departing, the loss will not be nearly as great as term limits critics will say.

   As to the choices among the term limit alternatives, the most rational approach, in my judgment, is embodied in House Joint Resolution 73 which I have offered and is the base text before us today. It provides a permanent 12-year limit on both the House and Senate with no retroactivity and silence on State premption. To provide lower limits for the House than for the Senate would mean that the House would become a weaker body vis-a-vis the Senate. Furthermore, a 6-year House limit does not provide sufficient time for a Member to become experienced enough to do a good job in serving as a chairman of a full committee or in a major leadership position in Congress. Shorter limits validate the critics' argument that term limits will lead to staff domination whereas 12 years virtually eliminates it.

Those who want to set a 12-year cap and leave it to the States to decide lesser limits are asking for a permanent hodgepodge of 6-,8-, and 12-year limits throughout the Nation which in the long run cannot help but be bad public policy. It is naive to assume that all States would eventually reach a uniform norm under the 12-year cap. Political reality says that some States would always have lower limits than others. If the Supreme Court rules in favor of the States in the current pending case, such a hodgepodge could exist even under House Joint Resolution 73, but others want to give States such a right regardless of the Court interpretation in the constitutional language. This simply does not make sense.

Some term limits supporters genuinely favor retroactivity, but most understand that in the current debate retroactivity is a mischievous tool of those who are opposed to limits. None of the 22 States that have adopted term limit initiatives have retroactivity. In Washington State where it was featured, the initiative lost, and a later one without it succeeded. As a practical matter retroactivity will cost votes on final passage and every vote is going to be needed to get to the 290 necessary to pass term limits in the House today. The retroactivity amendment will kill term limits. And I urge a vote against it.

Though the merits of each term limit proposal should be thoroughly debated, every Member of the House who truly supports term limits should put aside their differences.

And when we get, after the amending process, to vote on final passage, we need a yes vote. Better than 80 percent of the American people favor term limits, Democrats and Republicans alike are evenly divided. We are going to have 80 to 90 percent of the Republicans voting for it. If we just get 50 percent of the Democrats to do it, we can pass term limits today.

We need to have this healthy debate. Term limits are overdue. I urge a favorable vote for the final passage of term limits and this great historic debate.

Mr. FRANK of Massachusetts. Mr. Chairman, I yield myself 15 seconds.

I am sorry my friend did not yield to me. As he described the terrible things that happen to the attitude of members who have been here too long and if they have been here, especially after 12 years, I was going to ask him when in his 15 years of service this terrible thing happened to him. But I guess I wil have to wait for my answer until later.

Mr. Chairman, I yield 5 minutes to the gentleman from Wisconsin [Mr. OBEY].

Mr. OBEY. Mr. Chairman, I thank the gentleman for the time.

I think the greatest disservice that any public official can pay to the people he represents and to the democratic system is to cynically manipulate public frustrations and to then give their voters the impression that they are pretending to be for something which they really are opposing.

I think that is happening today. I think the greatest honor a public official can do to the people he represents is to deal honestly with them, especially when he has an honest disagreement with them.

In my view, voters are being treated to a cynical charade by the way this term limit proposition is being handled in the House today. For many years, many in the Republican leadership have told the public that they are for term limits in order to get votes, but then they unexpectedly came into power. They find themselves now in control, and they now have to produce what they promised.

Does anybody really believe that a Member who has served 16 years is sincere in saying he is for term limits when he continues to file for reelection every 2 years? If they were sincere, it seems to me all they would have to do is to demonstrate that sincerity by simply deciding not to run again.

The process today, in my view, is designed to kill term limits. It allows Members to pretend that they are opposed to term limits by voting for any one of the four propositions before the House. But because there are four propositions rather than one, it procedurally or virtually guarantees that there will be insufficient votes for any one of the four, thus enabling people to go home and say, "Oh, I voted for term limits, but * * *."

It just seems to me that that is a charade which does the public no great service.

I would also point out that the main term limits amendment does not even apply to most senior Members of this House, such as myself. It is a "let's pretend" process. We all understand that many of the sponsors of this proposal are in a very uncomfortable position. They promised something they never dreamed they would have to deliver on, and now I think we have an elaborate charade to pretend that they tried.

I do not think that does any real service to the American people. I think we ought to play it straight and lay out our views on this issue honestly. That is what I think the gentleman from Illinois has done today.

Appendix II

The text of the [Inglis] amendment and the vote on this amendment:

"SECTION 1. No person who has been elected for a full term to the Senate two times shall be eligible for election or appointment to the Senate. No person who has been elected for a full term to the House of Representatives three times shall be eligible for election to the House of Representatives.

SECTION 2. No person who has served as a Senator for more than three years of a term to which some other person was elected shall subsequently be eligible for election to the Senate more than once. No person who has served as a Representative for more than one year shall subsequently be eligible for election to the House of Representatives more than two times.

SECTION 3. No elector or service occurring before this article becomes operative shall be taken into account when determining eligibility for election under this article."

The vote was taken by electronic device, and there were - ayes 114, nays 316, not voting 4.

Appendix III

Lott's Promise: Shodily Kept

In October, 1997 Lott promised an early Spring '98 debate and by March 6 a vote on campaign finance legislation. The fiasco began on February 23rd. By February 26, the issue of campaign finance legislation was dead for this congressional year.

A filibuster of the McCain / Feingold bill (S. 25) could not be overcome. The Senate vote (51 to 48) failed to invoke cloture and essentially blocked the bill for a second time in the 105th Congress.

Why this rejection of the McCain /Feingold bill which would have banned so-called soft money; redefined express advocacy advertisements; required greater disclosure, and prohibited foreigners from making campaign contributions?

Moments after the rejection of the McCain / Feingold bill, the Senate also filibustered and failed to invoke cloture on Lott's Paycheck Protection Act. This bill (defeated by a cloture vote of 46 to 53) would have required unions to obtain prior written permission before using any portion of members' dues to pay for political activites.

Promises...promises...promises. End of story.

Appendix IV

Proposed Campaign Finance Reform Issues To Be Debated In Drafting A Bill To Restore The Rights Of The Elected And The Rights Of The Electorate

Campaign finance reform debate at both the national and the state levels should include the following:

-   whether to set limits for the campaign period at three months, twelve months, etc.;

-   whether to encourage networks to give free tv time to each candidate;

-   whether to set a ceiling on the paid time allowed each candidate;

-   whether to ban all soft money contributions (both dollars and in-kind);

-   whether PACS should support only candidates from the state in which the PAC is headquartered;

-   whether to allow inter-State campaign funding - for example, Vermont voters legislated that candidates from Vermont only accept campaign funds from Vermont voters and from Vermont PACS;

-   whether to allow only federal tax deductions for campaign contributions and disallow all State tax deductions for campaign contributions;

-   whether contributions to the campaign should be voluntary: never imposed or enforced by employers, unions, etc.;

-   whether to set new limits for contributions currently set: to individuals, $1,000; to the National Party, $20,000; in the aggregate per election cycle, $25,000;

-   whether to set limits for the candidate's personal spending per election cycle;

- whether to disallow issue-advocacy ads which support or oppose candidates;

- whether or not to set limits on terms served as House or Senate Committee Chairmen;

- whether to encourage the stock market principle as a way to monitor a policy shift which may be based on an industry's campaign contributions.

About the Author

Paulette G. Honeygosky is a world traveler and scholar. She was educated at Duquesne, Kingston, St. Louis, and Bonaventure Universities. Honeygosky has also worked extensively as a teacher, a human rights activist, and as an advocate for the elderly. Presently, she is a senior researcher with a legislative team in Washington, D.C.